Life Without Parole

Living in Prison Today

Second Edition

Victor Hassine
Inmate AM4737
Pennsylvania Department of Corrections

Edited by:

Thomas J. Bernard
Pennsylvania State University

Richard McCleary
University of California, Irvine

Richard A. Wright
Arkansas State University

Foreword by
John Irwin
San Francisco State University

Roxbury Publishing Company
Los Angeles, California

Library of Congress Cataloging-in-Publication Data

Hassine, Victor, 1955–
Life without parole: living in prison today / Victor Hassine; edited by Thomas
    J. Bernard, Richard McCleary, and Richard A. Wright; foreword by John Ir-
    win. — 2nd ed.
    p. cm.
Includes bibliographical references.
ISBN 1-891487-13-2 (alk. paper)
    1. Prisoners—Pennsylvania—Case Studies. 2. Hassine, Victor, 1955–. 3.
    Life imprisonment—Pennsylvania—Case studies. 4. Prisons—Pennsylva-
    nia—Case studies. 5. Graterford State Correctional Institution. I. Bernard,
    Thomas J. II. McCleary, Richard. III. Title.
HV9475.P2H37   1999
365'.6'0922748—dc21   98-19440
                                                                                CIP

LIFE WITHOUT PAROLE: LIVING IN PRISON TODAY
(SECOND EDITION)

Publisher and Editor: Claude Teweles
Copy Editor: Arlyne Lazerson
Production Editors: Carla Max-Ryan and Dawn VanDercreek
Production Assistants: Kate Shaffar, James Ballinger, and Cathy Yoo
Typography: Synergistic Data Systems
Cover Design: Marnie Kenney

Printed on acid-free paper in the United States of America. This paper meets the
standards for recycling of the Environmental Protection Agency.

ISBN: 1-891487-13-2

> *Note: All author royalties for this book are being donated directly to The Families*
> *of Murder Victims Program, a nonprofit organization affiliated with the Antivio-*
> *lence Partnership of Philadelphia, Pennsylvania, and the Pennsylvania Prison*
> *Society's Ted Klugman Memorial Fund. The Pennsylvania Prison Society is a*
> *nonprofit organization dedicated to prison education and reform.*

ROXBURY PUBLISHING COMPANY
P.O. Box 491044
Los Angeles, California 90049-9044
Tel: (310) 473-3312 • Fax: (310) 473-4490
Email: roxbury@crl.com

This book is dedicated to the memory of Ted "Tefka" Klugman, a good and courageous man who dedicated his life to helping those in need. The world has lost a hero while heaven has gained an angel.

A Needed New Additon
It first began in tragedy only to become a journey of love. With all my heart, forever, I do . . .

V.H.

About This Book

In 1981 law-school graduate Victor Hassine was sentenced to prison for life without parole for a capital offense. His updated book is an insightful look at conditions of confinement and prison life in America today, guiding the reader into the very essence of the prison experience. Hassine powerfully conveys the changes in prison life which have come about as a result of the use of drugs, prison overcrowding, and demographic changes in inmate populations. Topics covered include rape, prison gangs, prison violence, AIDS, homosexuality, and prison politics.

About the Second Edition

The First Edition of *Life Without Parole: Living in Prison Today*, was enthusiastically received. This Second Edition features four new chapters that explore crucial topics expanding on the First Edition—graphically documenting the extreme violence that is a part of everyday life in a men's maximum security prison:

New Chapters:

- Chapter 3, "Playing the Opposites," describes a common "game" that inmates play to get what they want in prison, requiring routine lying to staff members under the belief that prison officials always act against the best interests of inmates.

- Chapter 14, "Coach: A Changeling," offers an interview with a correctional officer turned criminal by the corruption and brutality that he observed while working in prison.

- Chapter 15, "The Dancing Man," is Victor Hassine's first-hand account of a violent and destructive prison riot.

- Chapter 17, "Prison Rape," candidly describes the strategies involved in sexual assaults on inmates.

- Chapter 20, "Conclusion: Runaway Train," has been significantly updated and revised.

A new Appendix offers details about the captial offense for which Hassine received a life-without-parole sentence. It also describes how the First Edition was received by inmates and correctional officials.

Contents

Part III: Op Ed

Acknowledgements

The success of the First Edition of this book has been a tremendously satisfying experience. I owe a lifetime of gratitude to a great many people who supported me, cared about me, believed in me, and encouraged me during these difficult prison years and while I was writing this book. You can't do time in prison alone and still expect to come out of it sane. I needed a lot of help from people on the outside to constantly remind me that I was still a worthwhile part of the American quilt.

I would like to start by thanking my father, mother, and brother who in many ways did this time with me so I would never have to feel completely alone. I hope the publication of this book will give them that sense of pride which I have not been able to offer since my incarceration. But for them I would have long ago lost this struggle to retain my dignity.

I would like to personally thank Deborah Anthony who saved my life.

From Graterford Penitentiary I would like to thank Larry Karlin for being the devoted friend I could always count on to be in my corner; Ted Klugman (Tefka), who was the first one to encourage me to write about my prison experiences and who introduced me to the Fortune Society and the Pen Prison Writing Contest; Phil and Frida Zelt, Catherine Sion, Itka Zigmantovitch, and many other prison volunteers who showed me friendship, kindness, and concern, which in turn gave me the strength and inspiration to write this book; Angus Love, the best, most honest, and committed lawyer I know, without whose dedication Pennsylvania prisons would be much worse places to be; and Irv Hommer, the radio talk-show host who showed me in no uncertain terms that many people out there really do care.

From Western Penitentiary I would like to thank Meyer and Sandra Tattelman, Sam Steinberg, and Rabbi Epstein—Jewish volunteers who managed to inspire hope in the most hopeless prison imaginable; Ken Davenport who, with the assistance of Nelson "Peepers" Mikesel, helped me to file and successfully litigate my conditions of confinement lawsuit against Western Penitentiary; Ed Feinstein, the lawyer whose skill and talent kept me many times from harm's way; and Bob Koehler, my college fraternity brother (Phi Alpha), who has stayed with me all these years.

From Rockview Penitentiary I would like to thank Rita Foderaro, a dear friend who believed in my talent and encouraged people to read my work; and two staff members, Mr. Sefchick and Mr. Davys, who provided me with the encouragement and support to write this book.

Many thanks to former Pennsylvania Commissioner of Corrections David Owens who tried diligently to change the Pennsylvania prison system for the better; former Commissioner of Corrections Joseph D. Lehman who gave not only his permission but his support for the writing of this book; the Pennsylvania Prison Society for having the courage and perseverance to demand a human face on the Pennsylvania Department of Corrections; the Fortune Society of New York for promoting the annual PEN American Prison Writing Competition, which was directly responsible for my decision to express myself through the written word.

Finally, a special thanks to the Superintendent of the State Correctional Institution at Rockview, Dr. Joseph F. Mazurkiewicz, for working so hard and unyieldingly to keep his prison safe and clean for its inmates. If I had been sent to Dr. Mazurkiewicz' prison fifteen years ago to serve my time, I probably would not have had very much to write about. And a very special thanks to editors Thomas J. Bernard, Richard McCleary, and Richard A. Wright for their patience and dedication to making this Second Edition possible. Lastly, my deepest gratitude to Sherry Truesdell of Truesdell Word Processing Services for her professionalism, honesty, and dependability; and to Roxbury's publisher, Claude Teweles, for his invaluable efforts in making this book a reality.

In addition, my publisher and I would like to offer thanks to the following individuals who were kind enough to offer their reactions to the First Edition and make suggestions for the Second Edition: Peter Benekos (*Mercyhurst College*), Marion Cockey

(*Towson University*), Phyllis Gerstenfeld (*California State University, Stanislaus*), Tara Gray (*New Mexico State University*), Clayton Hartjen (*Rutgers University*), William Harver (*University of Delaware*), Christopher Hensley (*Northern State University*), Mathew Karjirathinkal (*Texas A&M University*), Matthew Leone (*University of Nevada, Reno*), Lucien Lombardo (*Old Dominion University*), Javier Trevino (*Wheaton College*).

Foreword

John Irwin
San Francisco State University

Victor Hassine's *Life Without Parole* takes its place among a rather large array of descriptions of prison life written by prisoners. Some of these were written in the last century, but the majority of them came about in the last three decades, for the obvious reason that prisoners are becoming more and more literate. Some of the best of these are: *In the Belly of the Beast* by Jack Abbott; *A Sense of Freedom* by Jimmy Boyle (a British prisoner); *Tales from the Joint* by K. Hawkeye Gross; and *The Big Huey* by Greg Newbold (a New Zealand prisoner).

I think Hassine's book is most like Gross' *Tales from the Joint*, because both books were written by people who had little experience with the social worlds, mostly lower class, that supply prisons their inmates. *Life Without Parole*'s particular strength is that it is about large, contemporary prisons. Until reading this book, I hadn't seen any good prisoner descriptions about prisons today, after the extreme overcrowding and the violence between prisoners that have changed conditions so significantly. Hassine has a sharp eye for contemporary prison violence because he came to prison as an outsider, unfamiliar with the patterns and values of the thieves, hustlers, drug addicts, state-raised convicts, and gang bangers who populate the prison. At times, perhaps, Hassine accepts too readily other prisoners' fairly standard explanations for the way things are, but he is intelligent and frequently sees things clearly from his very different perspective (he is a law-school graduate).

All in all, *Life Without Parole* is a very valuable work on the contemporary prison, produced by an intelligent individual who has experienced prison first-hand for an extended period.

Preface

The Story Behind This Book

Thomas J. Bernard
Pennsylvania State University

In December 1992, I received a call from the local representative of the Pennsylvania Prison Society, a private, voluntary agency that works with prisoners. She wanted to know if I would address the Lifers Group at the State Correctional Institution at Rockview about future possibilities for the release of life-sentenced inmates. Rockview is located near Pennsylvania State University, where I teach criminal justice courses.

In Pennsylvania, "lifers" are inmates who have been sentenced to life without parole. What these lifers wanted to know was whether there was any hope that they might eventually get out of prison. For them, the only way out (other than death or escape) is to receive a commutation from the governor. Up until about 1980, commutations in Pennsylvania were treated somewhat like parole. There were hearings on the issue, so that those who applied for commutation had at least some but not very much hope that it might be granted.

With the recent shift to a "get-tough" approach to crime, however, this is no longer the case. In the first half of the 1970s, Pennsylvania averaged over 30 commutations per year. By the second half of the 1980s, that figure had dropped to just over one per year. Since his election in 1995, Pennsylvania Governor Tom Ridge has granted *no* commutation. At the same time, about 100 life-sentenced inmates have been coming into the state's system every year. So as a practical matter, life-sentenced inmates today can expect their requests for commutation to be denied, regardless of the circumstances of their crime, the length of time they have served, or their record and accomplishments since they have been in prison. This is not likely to change any time soon.

So my answer to the lifers' question was no. But I tried to couple that bleak message with a tiny glimmer of hope. Inmate population pressures in the Pennsylvania system, in my view, made it inevitable that a genuine consideration of commutation applications would eventually have to be resumed. There were simply too many life-sentenced inmates coming into the system, and the present commutation policy was too impractical to last forever.

If these inmates have nothing else in their lives, they have time. If they can do nothing else with their time, they can wait. The small shred of hope that I could give them was gratefully received. I was enthusiastically thanked for my presentation. Many smiling, desperately friendly faces were thrust into mine to tell me how much my talk meant to them.

* * * *

One of those friendly faces belonged to Victor Hassine, although I did not remember meeting him at the time. Then in August 1993, an envelope arrived in the mail containing three of the interviews that are included in this book. A letter from Victor proposed that I share this material with my students since, "if they are to make a meaningful contribution to the administration of justice in Pennsylvania, they need to know the truth about its operation." I wrote him a brief note of thanks and then set the envelope aside.

Eventually, I got around to reading the material carefully. To my surprise, the interviews provided strikingly vivid descriptions of inmates and life in prison that were remarkably well-written and deeply insightful. I was intrigued. After considerable thought, I came to the conclusion that this material might form the basis for a book about prison life. I decided to look into it further.

First, I had to find out if the Department of Corrections would allow a book to be written by an inmate. It was a very long time before I received an answer: inmates could indeed write books as part of their freedom of speech. By the time I received their reply, Roxbury Publishing Company had agreed to publish the book.

On February 28, 1994, I wrote Victor a letter to inform him that I had been working on a proposal for him, that the Department of Corrections had agreed to the book, and that a publisher was ready to offer him a contract if he still wanted to do it. It was the first time I had communicated with him since my note of thanks, because I did not want to offer any good news until all the pieces were in place, for fear of raising his hopes prematurely.

Victor's response was ecstatic. He readily agreed to all the arrangements and suggested that his royalties be split between a Philadelphia group called "Families of Murder Victims" and a special fund of the Pennsylvania Prison Society set up to honor his friend Ted Klugman.

"Families of Murder Victims" is a private, nonprofit agency housed in, but not affiliated with, the Philadelphia District Attorney's office. Its purpose is to help families of homicide victims cope with their grief and to assist them as their cases work their way through the legal system. Funding for the agency comes from the Victims of Crime Act, the Philadelphia District Attorney's office, and the United Way, as well as from private donations. The Pennsylvania Prison Society has been promoting correctional reform and social justice for more than two centuries. The group was founded in 1787, and held its first meeting in the home of Benjamin Franklin. The group now organizes visits to prisoners in many prisons across the state of Pennsylvania. Ted Klugman was a prison volunteer who visited Victor in Graterford Penitentiary and was the first person to encourage Victor to write about his prison experiences. The contract with Roxbury Publishing Company specifies that all of Victor's royalties go directly to and be split evenly between these groups.

In my view, the result of this process is a book that provides a penetrating and insightful look at prison life in America today. Whether you are for or against prison reform, whether you support or oppose the get-tough policy on criminals, this book will give you a first-hand experience of what prisons are really like—a revealing look at prison life from the *inside*.

We, as citizens of a democratic society, should know what prisons are all about. Our society makes an enormous investment in prisons as part of social policy. Before 1970, our imprisonment rate was relatively stable at around 100 sentenced inmates for every 100,000 Americans. In that year, we had about 200,000 inmates in federal and state adult prisons. But around 1970, the numbers began taking off. Each year since then, the total number of inmates has increased between 50,000 and 90,000. As of this writing, the most recent figures show that on June 30, 1997, the United States had 1,218,256 inmates in state and federal prisons, for a rate of 436 sentenced inmates for every 100,000 Americans.[1]

This rate of growth means that, at the end of every week, correctional administrators in this country have to find rooms and beds for over 1,000 more inmates in their prisons than they had at the beginning of that week. This task is almost impossible, and it has led to many of the problems described in this book.

As responsible citizens, we need to ask ourselves whether this enormous investment in prisons is a worthy social policy. I hope that Victor Hassine's book will help to stimulate debate over this very serious question.

---

1. Darrel K. Gilliard and Allen J. Beck. "Prison and Jail Inmates of Midyear 1997," *Bureau of Justice Statistics Bulletin* January 1998. Department of Justice, Bureau of Justice Statistics. Washington, DC: U.S. Government Printing Office.

About the Author

Born: June 20, 1955.

1956: Family exiled from Egypt for religious reasons.

1961: Family immigrated to Trenton, New Jersey.

1966: Became an American citizen.

1977: Graduated from Dickinson College in Carlisle, Pennsylvania, majoring in political science and history.

1980: June, graduated from New York Law School. November, arrested on an open charge of homicide.

1981: Convicted of first-degree murder and sent to SCI-Graterford.

1985: Helped to found the first prison synagogue.

1986: Helped to found the first Jewish Post-Release House. Filed conditions of confinement suit in Federal Court against SCI-Graterford to abolish double-celling. September, assaulted by an inmate and transferred to SCI-Pittsburgh.

1987: Filed conditions of confinement suit in Federal Court against SCI-Pittsburgh and Pennsylvania Department of Corrections.

1989: January, assaulted by an inmate and recovered in outside hospital. April, transferred from Pittsburgh hospital to SCI-Camp Hill. August, transferred to SCI-Rockview.

1990: Received Pennsylvania Prison Society's Inmate of the Year Award.

1996: Publication of the first edition of *Life Without Parole: Living in Prison Today*.

Editors' Note

The names of many of the inmates and prison employees described in this book have been changed to protect their identity.

Note to Instructors

The Pennsylvania Department of Corrections has authorized the author, Victor Hassine, to participate in telephone conferences with students who are using this book in the classroom. Teleconferences of this nature were successfully conducted with many adopters of the First Edition.

If a professor is interested in participating in such a teleconference, please contact Roxbury Publishing and we will forward this information to the author who will send you information regarding prison approvals, scheduling, and teleconference format.

Part I

Prison Life

Editors' Note

In this first section, the author introduces himself and describes the beginning of his life as a convict in prison. His first life, which is briefly summarized above in "About the Author," ended in 1981 at the gates of the State Correctional Institution at Graterford. His second life, which began in June of that year, is the focus of the next several chapters.

The following material will give the reader a keen insight into the nature of imprisonment from a personal perspective. Of course, different readers will form different impressions of prison life after reading this narrative. Consider the old parable of the two blind men who encountered an elephant. Grabbing its leg, one exclaimed, "An elephant is like a tree!" Grabbing its tail, the other said, "No, an elephant is like a snake!" We at least hope that readers' impressions tap the same vein, so that these writings offer a better understanding of the experience of incarceration.

Introduction

In 1980, Iran was holding Americans hostage and Cuban refugees were flooding into Florida. Interest rates were at a record high, digital watches were the rage, and Jimmy Carter was president.

For me, Victor Hassine, the first half of 1980 was a very good year. I was in love and seriously considering marriage. I graduated from New York Law School in June and soon after left my internship with the Manhattan District Attorney to join a small law firm in my adopted hometown of Trenton, New Jersey. I had a brand-new sports car and a very promising future. Given that I had arrived in the United States 19 years earlier as a non-English speaking refugee escaping religious persecution in Egypt, I felt that I was the textbook example of a man who had achieved the American dream.

All that changed in November of 1980, when I was arrested in Pennsylvania and held without bail on charges of conspiring in a man's death. The state sought the death penalty. In June of 1981, despite my vigorous denial of the charges, a jury of my peers found me guilty of first-degree murder.

Immediately following the verdict, I was confined to a small holding cell in the basement of the Courthouse, while the jury deliberated for two days on whether to condemn me to death by electrocution or sentence me to life imprisonment without parole. They ultimately decided on the latter choice.

My odyssey through the Pennsylvania penal system began in June of 1981 with my arrival at the State Correctional Institution at Graterford (SCI-Graterford), an immense, walled facility lurking in the quiet countryside northwest of Philadelphia. I expected to find myself in a rigid, structured environment designed to deter and punish, even though I half hoped that inmates were being coddled

3

as newspapers and TV reports had so often suggested. In any event, I assumed that everything was under control.

Within the first few weeks of incarceration, however, I began to realize that something was very wrong at Graterford. Fights were breaking out everywhere, the sale of drugs and contraband was commonplace, and it seemed as if everyone was carrying a weapon. Violence and corruption were rampant. Gangs ran the prison, terrorizing staff and inmates alike.

In my fourth month at Graterford, the prison was locked down while inmates with pistols and shotguns had a shootout with state police in a botched escape attempt that turned into a hostage situation. As the drama played itself out, I stayed in my cell for days, watching heavily armed state troopers rush back and forth.

In the months and years following the hostage crisis, prison life grew more violent, more uncontrolled, and a lot more crowded. I was in such a constant state of panic that I stopped feeling scared and just became desperate. I lived every moment as if it were my last, and I began to believe that I would never survive. I watched guards beating inmates and inmates beating and stabbing inmates and guards alike. I watched prison gangs rob and steal with impunity, while staff smuggled in contraband for sale on the black market. Rape was a common phenomenon of everyday life, as was sexual activity between inmates and staff members. There were no less than three riots in one 12-month period, all precipitated by electrical failures that caused blackouts on the housing blocks.

I had entered a system which seemed to exist only as a relentless generator of despair, corruption, and violence. I had become a "moment dweller" with no thoughts about the future. In my mind, I began to imagine a greeting on the wall: *Welcome to Graterford Penitentiary. Abandon all hope ye who enter here.*

Chapter 1

How I Became a Convict

Editors' Note

Nature versus nurture is a hot topic of debate among criminologists. The idea of an innate or genetic "propensity to crime," which dates back to the early nineteenth-century positivist school, fell out of favor some time after World War II. Although postwar criminologists were divided on the exact causes of criminal behavior, no thoughtful scholar espoused a theory of innate criminality. Likewise, postwar crime control programs focused on mechanisms that assumed free will, particularly rehabilitation and deterrence. After 30 years, theories of innate criminality began to return in the 1970s. Today, criminologists are divided on the topic.

The author, whether or not he was born a criminal—if he is a criminal at all—was certainly not a convict when he arrived at Graterford in 1981. No one is born a convict. The innocent and guilty alike learn to "become" convicts. Success in prison depends on how fast and how well the new inmate learns. This process of "becoming" is a major area of sociological research.

I have heard Graterford called The Farm, The Camp, The Fort, and Dodge City, but I have never heard it called safe. When I was in the county jail awaiting trial, I saw grown men cry because their counselors told them they were being transferred to Graterford.

G raterford State Prison, Pennsylvania's largest and most violent penal institution, was built in the early 1930s to hold all of the state's most violent prisoners. On June 14, 1981, while it could not contain all 8,000 or more of the state's most wanted, it certainly had enough room to hold me. Its steel-reinforced concrete wall measures four feet thick by 32 feet tall and encloses over 65 acres of land. Originally designed to hold eight separate cell blocks within its perimeter, Graterford ended up with only five. But these cell blocks are huge constructions, each containing 400 cells.

Everything inside appears as huge and massive as the wall itself. Each housing unit is a rectangular structure, measuring about 45 feet wide by three stories tall by 820 feet long (over twice the length of a football field), perpendicularly attached to a quarter-mile-long main corridor which measures about 20 feet wide by two stories high.

I knew none of this as I sat handcuffed and shackled in the back seat of the sheriff's car, waiting to be taken inside to begin serving my life-without-parole sentence. All I could see was a blur of dirty, grainy whiteness from the giant wall that dominated the landscape before me. It made me feel very small and insignificant, and very frightened.

A giant steel gate rose up to allow the sheriff's car to drive into Graterford's cavernous sallyport area, a fortified enclosure designed to control traffic. Once the gate fell shut, I was immediately hustled out of the car by some very large, serious-looking corrections officers. I knew I would have to submit to a cavity search, but it wasn't the strip search that dominated my memory of this event. It was the *noise*.

Since concrete and steel do not absorb sound, the clamor and voices from within just bounced around, crashing into each other to create a hollow, booming echo that never ended. It sounded as if someone had put a microphone inside a crowded locker room with the volume pumped up, broadcasting the noise all around the sallyport. It was this deafening background noise that would lull me to sleep at night and greet me in the morning for the next five years. Though I have been out of Graterford for many years now, its constant din still echoes in my ears.

The prison guards finished their search and escorted me up Graterford's main corridor, a dim, gloomy, 20-foot-wide by over 1,500-foot-long stretch. The lack of natural light and the damp, dungeon-like air in this place was oppressive. As I took one tentative step after another, I promised myself never to take bright and sunny places for granted again. Having just left the Courthouse hours before, I was so disoriented that I lost track of how far I had been walking.

Things changed with sudden permanence once I reached the central corridor gate that separated the administrative section from the prison proper. This was the first time I saw the faces, shapes, and shadows of the men who would become my future friends, enemies, and neighbors. They stared at me and I stared back, as scared as I had ever been in my entire life.

Once inside, I was walked through a gauntlet of desperate men. Their hot smell in the muggy corridor was as foul as their appearance. Most of them were wearing their "Graterford Tan," an ashen gray pallor. The discoloration of these distorted human forms represented the prison landscape. At Graterford you work, eat, sleep, and idle indoors. You never have to go outdoors unless you want to risk the sometimes deadly yard. Many inmates served their time like cave dwellers, never leaving Graterford's concrete and steel shelter.

My first impression was that most of these men brandished their scars and deformities like badges of honor. None of them seemed to have a full set of front teeth. Many bore prominently displayed tattoos of skulls or demons. They all seemed either too tall or too small, but none seemed right. Eyes were buggy, beady, squinted, or staring, but none were caring. Heads were too big, too small, pointed, swollen, or oblong, some with jutting foreheads, twisted noses, massive jaws, and gnarled hands. But none seemed human.

One could argue whether it was the look of these men that led them to prison or whether it was the prison that gave them their look. What tales of suffering their bodies told seemed to be of no concern to them. They were content to wear their scars openly like a warning, the way farmers use scarecrows to keep menacing birds away. Today I feel pity and compassion for those who have had to suffer so much pain and tragedy in one lifetime. But on that hot June day, all I wanted was to get away from these ugly creatures as quickly as possible. Just looking at them made me fear for my life. There was no pity or compassion in my heart then, because their grotesqueness made me forget they were human.

Now when I watch a new arrival walking "the gauntlet of desperate men," I can always sense his hopelessness. I know my staring is as horrifying to him as it was for me on my first day, and I know what I must look like to him.

Getting Classified

Toward the end of the main corridor I was shepherded into the shadowy expanse of yet another corridor. This led to the Clothing Room, a cold, damp place equipped with a tile-walled shower and an adjoining room where endless rows of mothballed clothes hung on racks like mismatched goods in a thrift shop.

My escort guard ordered me to "get naked" and surrender my personal effects to an inmate dressed in brown prison garb. I was still wearing my nice suit and tie from the Courthouse. As I stripped down, I handed the silent inmate the last vestiges of my social identity. He tossed them impatiently into an old cardboard box. After the guard conducted another "bend-over-and-stretch-'em" search, I was given delousing shampoo and ordered to shower.

As I stood naked and shivering after my shower, I was assigned two pairs of navy blue pants, two blue shirts, three T-shirts, three pairs of boxer shorts, three pairs of socks, a blue winter coat, a blue summer jacket, two towels, and a pair of brown shoes. Everything but the shoes and socks had "AM4737" boldly stamped in black. This number was my new, permanent identity.

Once I had dressed, I was taken to be fingerprinted and photographed, then escorted to E-Block, officially known as the Eastern Diagnostic and Classification Center (EDCC). Though Graterford had five cell blocks, only A- through D-Blocks were considered part of the prison. E-Block was treated as a separate facility, which inmates and staff called "Quarantine." Because all new receptions to

Quarantine were issued blue prison uniforms, they were labeled "Blues." The general population inmates who wore brown uniforms were referred to as "Browns." Contact between Blues and Browns was strictly forbidden.

Soon I found myself before the E-Block Sergeant's desk, wearing my new blue uniform, cradling my belongings, and waiting for whatever came next. The Sergeant walked me to a room full of bedding. There another inmate in brown dropped a rolled-up mattress on my shoulder. Inside it were stuffed a blanket, pillow, metal cup, plastic knife, fork, and spoon, a pack of rolling tobacco, soap, toothbrush, toothpaste, and a disposable razor.

Awkwardly balancing the mattress roll on my shoulder with one arm and carrying my prison-issued clothes with the other, I followed the Sergeant down a flight of stairs to my cell on one of the bottom ranges. The moment I twisted my body and cargo sideways into the dark, narrow cell, the Sergeant slid the door shut and disappeared from sight.

The next two days were spent in the prison's infirmary for shots and a complete medical examination. While it was a doctor who examined me, it was an inmate who drew my blood and wrote down my medical history. Since the infirmary was also used by Browns from general population, a guard followed me and the other receptions everywhere we went. This constant surveillance had me wondering why we were so heavily guarded.

I later learned that any exposure of Browns to Blues was closely watched by the staff. One reason was that, since they had more liberties than the new arrivals, Browns often tried to barter privileges with Blues. For example, a pack of cigarettes could buy extra phone time or a library pass; and for a pack a day, you could rent a TV or a radio. Also, some Browns would sexually exploit weaker Blues. Almost all of them were point men for prison gangs, who reported back on the new prospects among Blues for possible gang membership or future victimization.

After I completed the medical examination process, there were about two weeks of idleness. Finally I was taken to an Examination Room on the block for a series of written psychological and literacy tests. There was no supervision in this room, and the testing process took about two days.

Two months of more idleness followed as I waited to be interviewed by my counselor. There were over 400 inmates on E-Block and many fights. It seemed as if every time the block was let out into the yard, a fight would break out somewhere. From my experience, when convicts are let loose after being locked up for long periods of time, aggressive behavior is an immediate and natural consequence.

To occupy time, people played cards and worked out. It was during these idle days in classification that longstanding friendships and alliances were made and when inmates distinguished the weak from the strong—predators from victims.

The first impressions I made on others during classification have stayed with me in prison ever since. Since I was not a career criminal, I was initially viewed as a "square john": a middle-class outsider with no experience of the social world of inmates. To both my advantage and disadvantage, I was seeing everything through the eyes of a foreigner, making many foolish mistakes yet gaining just as many unique insights into their world.

When I was finally called in for my interview, the counselor examined my test results and asked me a minimum of questions about my conviction and sentence. The interview took only 10 to 15 minutes.

Two weeks later, I was summoned to appear before the Classification Committee. Sitting before a counselor, the block Sergeant, and a Major of the Guards, I was asked what prison I wanted to go to and why. I could only suggest Graterford since I didn't think other prisons would be any better or worse. Then I waited outside while they reviewed my file. Within a few minutes, I was called back and informed that I had been classified to Graterford. Just before I left, the Major added in a pleasant voice, "You'll be working for me."

At the time I didn't consider the significance of my job assignment. I was too relieved to know that the tortuous classification ordeal was finally over. A few days later, I traded in my blues for browns and moved off Quarantine into the general population.

To me and most of the others, as I later discovered, classification was a total waste of time. While different prisons in Pennsylvania purportedly provided different types of rehabilitation programs meant to serve the needs of various kinds of offenders, in reality it seemed that only three considerations were used to determine a convict's ultimate destination: (1) race, (2) hometown, and (3) availability of cell space. At the time, most of the minority inmates in the state were classified to Graterford or Western Penitentiary. The other seven prisons consisted of mostly white inmates under an all-white civilian staff.

From the inmate point of view, the testing was an utter sham. For one thing, the written tests were given to everyone without even determining who could read or write. The written tests I took were in an unsupervised room with about 30 other men, most of whom just picked answers at random or copied them from someone else.

Because the officials seemed flippant about the tests, inmates tended to see their results only as a tool of manipulation. Under this assumption, many men had developed theories on how to answer the test questions. Some felt it was best to copy from the brightest men in order to improve their chances at getting a clerk's job over kitchen or laundry duty. Others felt they should give lunatic answers so they could be medically released from work altogether. Still others gave no answers at all and faked illiteracy. Such men reasoned that they could enroll in school and appear to do extremely well, thereby fooling the parole board into believing they had worked hard to make a positive change in their lives. All these connivances were based on the inmates' understanding that they were being conned as much as they were doing the conning.

Getting Dug In

Inmates serving long sentences preferred to lock at Graterford because, even though it was violent, it afforded them the most personal liberty. This was so because the more violent a prison is, the more reluctant guards are to enforce petty rules for fear of being assaulted.

Once I was classified to Graterford, I had to move my belongings, along with my mattress, blanket, and pillow, to B-Block. This was a working block, reserved only for those inmates who had been assigned a job. My assignment turned out to be a fortuitous clerical job in the Major of the Guards' office. All my belongings were fit into a single shopping bag which I carried in one hand, while my rolled-up mattress was once again toted on my shoulder. I walked down the long main corridor to B-Block, my new home. Though it mirrored the design of E-Block, it was considerably less crowded and noisy. Comparatively, this hell seemed more like heaven to me.

The first thing I noticed was that the men on B-Block were much older than most of those on the classification block. These were the "Old Heads" of the prison, inmates who had done a long stretch. When I arrived at my assigned cell, I quickly signed in at the Block Sergeant's desk and requested cleaning supplies. Then I spent the morning scrubbing down every inch of my cell. By noon count I was able to lie down on my bed, smoke a cigarette, and consider what I was going to do next.

My cell measured about six feet by 12 with a ten-foot high ceiling, from which dangled a single light bulb with a drawstring switch. For furniture, I had a flat, hard steel bed and a steel desk and chair which had been assembled as one unit. The mandatory toilet afforded a sink directly above it with a steel medicine cabinet above that. High over the toilet was a rusty radiator which served as my only source of heat in the winter. Finally, I had a flimsy wooden foot locker with a hasp that could be locked with a commissary-bought combination lock.

My cell entrance was a solid steel sliding door with a fixed glass window on the top quarter. On the opposite wall was a window that could be manually opened and closed, just a little. The concrete walls were painted a dingy off-white and adorned with graffiti and cigarette stains.

Despite the grim accommodations, this was home. I was due to report to work the next morning and I could feel myself getting dug in. In prison it doesn't take much to make a man happy: food, some quiet, a good book, a job, and enough heat in the winter. That day I was happy just to be able to lie on that hard bed with a 70-watt light bulb glaring in my face. I felt the worst was over. I could now begin to serve my time.

Escape From Reality

Like most first-time arrivals to Graterford, I was only preoccupied with survival and how to avoid becoming the victim of violence. This sudden refocusing of attention led me to change my habits, my personality, and even my values. With these changes came a new way of viewing the world as a place of unrelenting fear.

If I made eye contact with a stranger, I would feel threatened. An unexpected smile could mean trouble. A man in uniform was not a friend. Being kind was a weakness. Viciousness and recklessness were to be respected and admired. Oddly enough, these changes were in some way comforting. In the struggle to survive, it was easier to distrust everyone than to believe in their inherent goodness.

Danger became a determining factor of the changes in my attitude and personality. When there was general movement in the prison, for example, the main corridor would fill with hundreds of inmates in transit. This made the corridor an extremely dangerous place to be. I was more likely to see a stabbing than a guard on duty.

The cell blocks were just as insecure. A guard at one end of a cell block could not identify anyone at the other end; the distance of 700 feet was just too great. Because of their fear of being assaulted where no one could see them, many block guards never patrolled the inner perimeter and spent most of their time avoiding conflicts at all cost, even turning the other way.

By the time I had settled in, however, I found myself feeling safe enough to think beyond the moment. This was something I had not been able to do since my arrest. Unfortunately, this new sense of security brought with it the "sleeping phase." I began to sleep 12 to 14 hours a day. My whole life consisted of eating, working, and sleeping. I never dreamed. I only tried to stay unconscious for as long as I possibly could.

Though I had no way of knowing it at the time, I had entered a very common prison-adjustment phase. So common, in fact, that walking in on a newcomer while he sleeps is the most practiced technique of cell thieves and rapists. In Graterford, a man who spends too much time in bed sends the same signal as that of a bleeding fish in shark-infested waters.

"You can't be sleeping all the time," cautioned my chess partner one day, waking me to play a game. "You can't sleep away your sentence. In here, you have to stay awake to stay alive."

He was right, and I knew it. So I resolved to keep myself busy. I took up reading and painting as hobbies. I was allowed to buy almost as many books, magazines, and newspapers as I wanted, as well as canvasses, brushes, and paints. Self-help was encouraged so long as you could pay for it yourself.

Soon I was reading everything I could get my hands on and painting well into the wee hours of the morning. My cell became crowded with books, magazines, canvasses, newspapers, and even an easel. I went so far as to rig up extra lighting, hang pictures, and buy throw rugs for the cement floor. I had successfully transformed my cell into a cluttered boarding-house room.

Like some literary critic and master artist, I was so deeply sub-merged in my hobbies that I became as obsessed as a man digging his way to freedom. But I was no literary critic and certainly no artist. I was just another lifer trying to escape the real world.

"You have to spend more time out of that cell, Victor," insisted my chess mate and only friend at that time. "It's not healthy to do a 'bit' [time] like that. Look at your cell, you have junk everywhere. You even have lights on your wall that look like they belong in a room somewhere else."

"I'm just getting dug in," I replied in defense, annoyed that my efforts at avoiding reality had been detected.

"This isn't getting dug in, this is foolishness. You're in a peni-tentiary—a tough one. You should never try to forget that. Never try to make yourself believe you're somewhere else. Do you know what a lit match could do to this cell?"

His words struck an unnerving chord. Only a few months ear-lier, I had watched a man whose cell across the way had been deliberately set on fire. He had screamed and banged helplessly on his locked door, flames dancing around him, biting at his flesh. Through his cell window, I could see billowing black smoke enve-lope his pleading, twisted, horrified face until he disappeared. It had taken some time before guards responded to his screams.

The very next day I gave away my books, magazines, news-papers, art supplies, and my easel. I knew I had to fight as hard for my safety as I did for my sanity.

Prison Slang

As a child immigrant who neither spoke nor understood Eng-lish, I once had to face the strange, intimidating world of the Ameri-can school system. But I overcame my fear of the unfamiliar because of my strong desire to adapt to a community of classmates. I wanted desperately to belong and to speak their language.

Likewise, from the outset of my term in Graterford I once again found myself in a frightening world where I couldn't understand the language or the behavior of its inhabitants. I felt that same desperate urge to belong to a community of inmates in the strange, new world of the American penal system. Everyone in prison—staff and inmates alike—seemed to know each other not only personally but intimately. They laughed and interacted like siblings, even during exchanges of anger. This strong familiarity gave the population of Graterford the appearance of one big clan. I wanted to be accepted by this clan, to know its secrets, and to speak its language.

One of the first things I knew I had to do was to adapt myself to the pervasive use of jailhouse slang by both inmates and staff. The tenor of this prison lingo was generally vulgar and aggressive, expressed with self-important arrogance. Yet at the same time it exhibited an unbridled honesty that implied a certain unconditional tolerance for the opinions and beliefs of others.

The first column below provides some examples of prison slang that might be heard on any given day in Graterford. The second column is the non-slang English version. Because these examples are condensed, the slang is expressed in a somewhat exaggerated form. These are just brief samples from the vast repertoire of expressions used in prisons today.

Graterford Version	*English Version*
Three homeys played a tip and did a B & E on the humbug. Dudes were stick-up boys, not back-door boosters, so they weren't down with it. Turns out to be a fat take. They find the stash and it's full of gold, rocks, paper, and cash money.	Three neighborhood friends followed up on a tipster's information and committed a house burglary on a sudden impulse. These men were armed robbers and not burglars so they were not familiar with the business. As it turned out, they stole a lot of money. They found a cache full of gold, precious stones, negotiable checks, and cash.
After breaking down the tip man, the cutees get to breaking down the gapper, when one of the homeys throws shit into the game and pulls out a gat, talking about,	After the man who tipped them off about the house was paid off, the three partners began to divide the money. One of them complicated matters by pulling a gun,

"I ain't breaking down with no lames." He plucks one dude and goes to capping the other, but ain't nothing slow about home boy and he breaks camp.

Now cutee's fast but he's a trembler, he ain't got no ticker for this kind of drama. He gets to dry snitching to the police, talking about, "Officer, I heard some shooting at such and such a place and so and so might know something about it." Police bust the dude with the gapper and the gat. He ends up taking 12 in the box but pulls a life sentence with a nickel to a dime running wild.

Dude caught a bad break on a good score. If he'd broke down with his homeys, instead of pulling that slimy shit, he'd be living large.

saying, "I'm not sharing any money with losers." He killed one man, but the other one was faster and managed to get away.

While the man who escaped was fast, he was frightened and didn't have the courage to deal with this kind of situation. He went to the police and hinted about the shooter's acts by saying, "Officer, I heard some shooting at such and such a place and so and so might know something about it." The police ended up arresting the shooter with the money and the gun. He had a jury trial but was found guilty and received a life sentence with a five-to-ten-year sentence running consecutive to the life sentence.

The man had bad luck during a big robbery. If he had shared the money with his friends, instead of being underhanded, he would be living prosperously.

Chapter 2

Things Missed

Editors' Note

"Punishment" is a central theme of the prison experience and, not surprisingly, a constant topic of debate. At the most abstract level, criminologists often argue whether punishment serves higher-level social functions. Does punishment reinforce social bonds, for example, as Durkheim argued? At a more pragmatic level, criminologists debate the effectiveness of punishment. Does punishment deter criminal behavior, for example, either by the person being punished (specific deterrence) or in others (general deterrence)? Within this debate, it is important to remember that the first American prisons, built in the late eighteenth century, were designed to replace punishments that were deemed inhumane—whipping, maiming, and hanging. When punishments were used in early American prisons, moreover, they were explicit and independent of imprisonment. The "punishments" that the author describes in this chapter, on the other hand, are implicit; that is, they are part and parcel of the prison experience. Readers may wonder whether the implicit punishments are any better or worse than the explicit punishments that prisons were designed to replace.

Punishments for Misconduct

Reprimand and Warning

A warning from the Hearing Examiner not to do it again, "or else!"

Loss of Privilege

Suspension of privileges for a given period of time. These privileges include visiting, phone calls, commissary, yard, work, and television.

Cell Restriction

Confinement to one's cell except for meal lines and two hours per day recreation on the block, and loss of job. All other privileges are left intact unless specifically suspended.

Double-lock Feed-in

Confined to one's cell except for two hours recreation on the block and three showers per week. Loss of job, all privileges suspended or curtailed, and three full meals in the cell.

Disciplinary Custody

The Hole, or "Siberia." Solitary confinement in the isolation unit (Restrictive Housing Unit, or RHU) with all privileges suspended or curtailed. Three full meals in the RHU cell, and two hours recreation per day.

One of the more subtle ways a prison punishes is by its neglect of a man's need for things, both the abstract (e.g., his freedom) and the tangible (e.g., his personal property). From the very start, I began missing both. Just when I would get accustomed to doing without old things, I would start to miss new things. It was almost as if prison life had created a newfound desire in me to miss something all the time.

At first, I missed the obvious: sex, love, family, and friends. But it wasn't long before I stopped missing these things and started focusing on the next wave of things I no longer had: privacy, quiet, and peace of mind, intangibles that I have never stopped missing to this day.

There are no trees in the great walled fortress of Graterford and very few shrubs. In fact, there isn't much of anything green that hasn't been painted green. Also, the prison is designed so that you can never get an unobstructed view of anything. Walls keep getting in the way.

Occasionally when I had to make trips outside the prison for court appearances or doctors' visits, I would sit in the prison van enraptured by the trees whizzing past. The brightness and the beautiful colors of everything around me made every outside trip an exciting experience. I know of several men who filed lawsuits or feigned illnesses just to get "some streets."

Well aware of this, the administration would try to make such trips as uncomfortable as possible. They would handcuff and shackle traveling inmates and strip-search every man coming and going, even though he never left the sight of an officer. They would make certain that an inmate wore ill-fitting clothes that were dirty, torn, and extremely uncomfortable. In the winter they had only summer clothes available and only winter garments in the summer. For a while they even required a man to be locked in his cell the day before making such a trip.

But no amount of discouragement worked. Inmates loved these trips, because they reminded them of all the things they missed. Personally, I always came back from each trip remembering the trees, the beautiful women, and all the joys of the outside world. Longing for these things made me take a lot of risks in my efforts to reclaim even the most insignificant of things that I once had taken for granted.

Having It My Way

My first misconduct at Graterford resulted from missing one of life's simplest pleasures: a fresh-cooked hamburger. I had just come out of classification and started working the 12-to-8 p.m. shift as a clerk in the Major of the Guards' office, which was off the main corridor between E and D Block. One day a contraband sandwich merchant, or "swag man," walked into the office and offered me a ten-pound bag of frozen ground beef for a pack of cigarettes. I had no way of cooking it, but for another pack I could get a hot plate. I began to imagine myself biting into a hot, juicy burger grilled to perfection. I bought the contraband beef, which was a bargain considering that a pack of cigarettes at that time cost only 50 cents in the commissary.

A senior clerk helped me out by talking to an inmate kitchen worker, who quickly produced the heating element of an electric coffee urn and an aluminum cookie pan, both hidden in the lining of his oversized prison-issued coat. For only one more cigarette pack, he scrounged up hamburger buns, chopped onions, butter, sliced cheese, ketchup, mustard, and two bricks to hold the cookie pan over the heating element.

That evening when the meat had finally thawed, my co-conspirators and I set up a makeshift grill in the Major's bathroom. We fashioned burger patties and started frying the hamburgers as soon as movement in the main corridor had ended.

It was the onions that did us in. The aroma of sauted onions in butter was so strong that it attracted a guard stationed some 300 feet away. He followed the aroma to its origin and asked us for a burger. We were more than happy to share with him, and he was eating it as he left the office, which made us all sigh with relief.

A few minutes later, a Search Team raided us and confiscated everything. They had been tipped off when the previous guard offered one of them a bite of his tasty burger. When they asked him where he had gotten it, he simply told them. Apparently the members of the Search Team were not as impressed with our resourcefulness.

In the early 1980s, Graterford introduced the Search Team, or "A Team," as a special two-man guard squad whose sole function was to conduct cell searches and pat downs. Not even the block officers knew who or when they would strike. Whenever a Search Team entered a block, an inmate would call out, "Search Team up!" Inmates at the end of the block would immediately hide their contraband. Because it took so long for the team to make it down the long block, contraband was able to be moved constantly without detection.

Given that our hamburger caper took place in the Major's office, however, we didn't have that advantage. We were all issued misconduct reports for the possession of contraband. Following a misconduct hearing, I was found guilty, removed from my job, and forced to pay for the food. I was also confined to my cell for 60 days, allowed out only two hours per day for recreation on the block. As shown at the beginning of this chapter, "cell restriction" is classified as a third-level punishment for misconduct.

My biggest mistake in this case was my naiveté. Until the Search Team had confiscated the burgers, I thought that such activity was merely business as usual at Graterford. I had only been in general population for about a month, and things developed with such effortless ease that I hadn't taken what I had done very seriously. For many years afterward, my prison handle became "Burger King," even though I had never gotten a chance to taste the object of my crime.

The Hole

Every prison attempts to gain a specific end in some way, be it deterrence, punishment, and/or rehabilitation. What makes a prison unnatural is the way it tries to achieve that end. For example, a prison imposes communal existence on loners and others who would normally segregate themselves from each other, such as blacks and whites. And, despite the endless promulgation of rules, their enforcement is so arbitrary that inmates live in a constant state of uncertainty.

Disciplinary segregation, or the "Hole," serves no ultimate end but to deprive a man of *all* things except the bare necessities of survival. It is a highly contradictory experience for every inmate. To some it is punishment, to others it is safety, and to still others it is just another way to do time. Furthermore, solitary confinement is completely contrary to a prison's principle of imposed communal living.

From my own experiences in the Hole, the only thing that saved me from falling into the great abyss that separates the sane from the insane was the fact that I could read. For the illiterate, solitary confinement is a one-way ticket to madness.

While I was in the Hole, I discovered illiterate inmates who managed to alter their mental states enough to make the Hole their home, even convincing themselves that they preferred the "independence" of the Hole. Generally, they adapted to their environment in one of two ways: they totally threw themselves at the mercy of the guards in order to satisfy their hunger for conversation, or they communicated with other Hole residents by shouting from cell to cell for hours at a time. As I spent my time reading, I could hear their loud chatter as they tried to hang onto some last vestige of sanity.

One important thing that the Hole made me realize was how essential education should be to a prison system. I came to this conclusion because it seemed that only a literate inmate can truly know and understand the punishment attached to his wrongful acts.

At one point I had an opportunity to talk with an illiterate young man in the cell next to mine. He was doing disciplinary time for fighting. During most of his waking hours, he would sit on the floor next to the bars of his cell and talk to me or anyone else about everything and nothing. I knew he could not read so I understood what he was doing and tolerated his constant intrusion into my solitary world of reading.

One day he asked me what day it was and how many more days he had to go. The first thing I always did in the Hole was to keep some kind of a calendar, lest they forget to let me out on time. After some quick math, I told him he had only 28 days left. He then asked when that would be. I didn't understand the question, until he explained that he wanted to know how many more Sundays he would have to do.

This young man's illiteracy was so profound that he had no concept of time. To him the number 28 was as remote as the number 1,000,000. So if he didn't understand the length of his disciplinary time, there was no way he could fully comprehend the time the courts had given him to serve his sentence in prison.

If a man's illiteracy prevented him from understanding relative lengths of time, then what other things couldn't he understand? How could he ever possibly be deterred if he can only fathom the consequences of his actions *after* he has experienced them? Literacy should be high on the critical list of missed things for such a man, especially if he doesn't even know what he's missing.

After my conversation with my young Hole neighbor, I didn't give it much more thought. I immersed myself back into my book, but only after I checked my pencil-marked calendar and thanked God for the few remaining days I had left. I also thanked God for allowing me to be literate enough to understand time, space, and the Hole.

The Inmate's Dilemma

The foremost tangible things missed by inmates are their stolen personal possessions, particularly considering how little they're permitted to keep in their cells. At Graterford, there was always an epidemic of cell thefts.

Fortunately for me, everybody on B-Block where I lived had jobs. This meant that most of them made enough money to shop at the commissary every week. Some of them had manufacturing jobs in Correctional Industries, such as weaving, shoemaking, or tailoring, and could make well over a 100 dollars a month if they worked overtime. By prison standards this was considered to be a small fortune.

Total employment meant that there was not a major theft problem on B-Block at the time. This was a great relief to me, not because I didn't expect to get some of my things stolen, but because I didn't want to deal with the inevitability of catching some thief in the act.

In the life of an inmate, if you catch someone stealing from you, you're compelled to deal with it physically. This is not because you want to or you think it's the right thing to do, but because you absolutely must. If someone steals from you and you decide to report him to the guards, all that will happen is that the thief will go to the Hole for a while. Soon he'll be back in population and ready to seek revenge. Revenge in prison can take place years down the road. It generally occurs when you are vulnerable and the avenger happens to be around. This reality will leave you constantly looking over your shoulder. Additionally, involving the guards will get you the reputation as a "snitch," which means you will be physically challenged by inmates seeking to make a reputation or pass their own "snitch" label onto you.

If you choose to ignore the theft, the man will steal from you again and tell his friends, who in turn will also steal from you. Eventually, you will be challenged for more than just minor belongings. This "Inmate's Dilemma" is precisely why most men in prison hope they never have to deal with a sloppy cell thief. Unfortunately, many men who were caught stealing on the streets will just as easily get caught stealing in prison.

By 1982, there was no way an inmate could lock his own cell at Graterford. Cells were all locked or opened simultaneously at given intervals by the pulling of a single lever. At 6:00 a.m., for example, all the cells on the block were levered open so each inmate could open and close his own cell during breakfast. Five minutes after last call for breakfast, the levers were pulled again to lock all the doors. If you returned late from breakfast, you would have to wait for all the cells to be levered open again before you could re-enter your cell. In case of an emergency, each guard had a key which could override the lever and let you in. But asking a guard to key you in was like asking for a key out of the prison.

This process of opening and closing all doors at once was repeated at 8:00 a.m. for work lines and yard line; then again at 11:00 a.m. for count; at noon for lunch; at 5:00 p.m. for count; at 6:00 p.m. for supper; at 6:30 p.m. for block out, yard out, or work lines; then finally at 9:00 p.m. for final count and lockdown. Every one of us religiously followed this schedule because we always wanted to be at our cells when they opened up. Otherwise, we stood the chance of losing everything of value.

To combat theft, I arranged a neighborhood-watch system with my neighbors to look out for my cell when I wasn't there and vice versa. But for the most part it was every man for himself. From time to time I would return to my cell and discover things missing.

Fortunately I have never had to face the Inmate's Dilemma, but many others have and the consequences were brutal. There is no walking away in Graterford—the walls see to that—so either the intruder or the victim ends up seriously hurt.

One example of a cell confrontation involved not a cell thief but a Peeping Tom. One of my cell-block neighbors was Dip, a cocky body builder with an imposing physique. He was convinced that the mere sight of his impressive frame would deter anyone from ever messing with him. While other inmates ran to their cells when the levers were thrown to protect their belongings, Dip never bothered.

Then one day Dip returned to his cell from a shower, wearing only a towel around his nakedness. To his shock, he found an inmate hiding under his bed with an exposed erection, trying to watch him undress. Dip was so caught off guard that the intruder simply walked out, blowing him a kiss as he turned to run off the block. Once he had recovered his senses, Dip got very mad. He dressed himself for combat and stormed down the block to find the man who had challenged his manhood. The jeers and heckles of neighboring inmates only served to deepen his rage.

But the moment Dip stepped into the main corridor, the kiss blower was waiting with some friends. Dip was stabbed several times with homemade knifes. Lucky for him, his injuries were only "Graterford wounds," meaning that his vital parts were still intact. By the time guards had made it to the scene, the attackers were gone, one of their knives was left behind, and bleeding Dip was locked up—charged with possession of the weapon that had been used to stab him.

For the most part, the prison administration did nothing to curb cell thefts or invasion of cell privacy. Some guards also seemed to think that these thefts and intrusions were part of the punishment of prison. In due time, however, the administration's failure to provide adequate safety and security would have far-reaching consequences.

Throughout 1981 and 1982, inmates petitioned, begged, and even threatened in their efforts to convince the administration to provide some means by which inmates could lock their own cells. The administration rejected these requests, claiming that cells were secure enough. If the administration had conceded to such requests, it would have been a tacit admission that they did not have control over their own prison.

By 1982, Graterford's general population rose to over 2,000. Every cell in the general population blocks was occupied and in the classification block the new receptions were already being double-celled. There were not enough jobs to go around now, so many men sat idle on B-Block. This resulted in more theft, which in turn led to more fights and more stabbings.

The Day of Locking Cells

As thievery increased, gangs flourished. Some gangs were formed to steal, others to defend against burglaries and robberies. Since B-Block was comprised mostly of working inmates, the fighting was not as frequent. But D and C Blocks were virtual war zones. There were so many fights and retaliations that guards were getting injured in the melees.

Only then did the administration take action. Holes were drilled in the cell-door tracks so that any cell could be locked from the outside with a padlock, even when the master lever was opened. The commissary began selling padlocks that could fit in the hole. There was a general feeling of relief, because now we could secure our belongings. It seemed less likely now that we would ever have to deal with the Inmate's Dilemma—or so we thought.

Once gangs form in a prison, they're hard to break up. When a group of cell thieves join together, no lock can stop them. Their incentive had increased now as well, especially since this new sense of security encouraged inmates to keep more valuable goods in their cells.

To get around the new cell locks, thieves simply changed their techniques. The problem that remained was that when the master lever was open and the inmate was inside his cell, he could not lock himself inside the cell. Instead of waiting until an inmate left his cell, a gang would simply rush into the cell while he was sleeping or using the commode. This resulted in even more fights and stabbings. Burglary is one thing, but strong-armed robbery demands an immediate and violent response. As the number of robberies and assaults surged, the new jailhouse wisdom was that you should always be awake and ready to fight when cells were opened, and that you should use the commode only when your cell was locked.

Some prisoners began fashioning weapons that could withstand a shakedown. For example, they would keep wooden floor brushes in their cells. Made of solid oak, these heavy brushes could knock a man unconscious. Since they were prison issue, they weren't considered contraband. If a guard found one in your cell, all he could do was confiscate it or order you to return it to the Block Sergeant. Ironically, the heavy-duty combination locks sold in the commissary served as another shakedown-proof weapon. Placed in a sock, this weapon could be more effective than most homemade knives.

The ultimate defense against unwanted intruders was getting a hole drilled on the *inside* of your door. A bolt secured in this hole prevented the door from being opened, so you could now lock your cell from the inside as well as from the outside. The staff objected to this hole on the grounds that an inmate could barricade himself in his cell so it could only be opened with a cutting torch. If a guard saw a hole on the inside of your door, he might plug it up with metal solder, but it was easy enough to get another hole drilled.

A combination lock on the inside door-jamb hole rendered a man's cell fairly secure. The ability to keep more property without being restricted to their cells freed inmates from the routine of protecting their belongings. This meant more socialization, recreation, and work. It also meant the gangs would have to change their style of doing business once again. The treasures now accumulating in the cells were just too much to resist.

Chapter 3

Playing the Opposites

Editors' Note

In a well-known study of mental hospitals, sociologist Erving Goffman noted that patients adopt unique strategies and role adjustments to cope with the stigma of institutionalization. One such adjustment is "playing it cool," a strategy that involves telling staff members to their faces what they want to hear, while condemning and ridiculing them behind their backs. In the process of "putting one over" on the staff, patients reaffirm each others' opinions and feelings of self-worth.

Goffman speculated that the pains of imprisonment produce similar role adjustments among inmates. In this chapter, Hassine confirms this view by describing a common strategy called "playing the opposites." Inmates who play the opposites routinely lie to staff members when asked to express a desire or a preference. This game assumes that prison officials inevitably use their immense authority against the best interests of prisoners; misleading staff members is the only way for inmates to get what they want.

Readers should keep in mind, however, that playing the opposites has a ruinous side-effect: it advances the general stereotypes held by prison officials that most inmates are deceitful, manipulative, and untrustworthy. Furthermore, inmates skilled in this ruse almost certainly will experience problems coping with authority when released from prison.

> "What we've got here is failure to communicate!"
> —Prison chain gang captain,
> played by Strother Martin
> *Cool Hand Luke*
> Warner Brothers, 1967

Shortly after I arrived at Graterford, I discovered that my fellow inmates made a point of "playing the opposites." This game involves reverse psychology, where prisoners state the opposite of their actual feelings when asked by someone in authority to voice a preference or an opinion. A common occasion for playing the opposites is when an inmate is being interviewed by a counselor or employment officer for a job assignment. Naturally, some work details are favored over others, so experienced inmates will do whatever they can to secure a desirable job.

Some inmates will state their real job preferences and then try to influence assignments by summarizing their qualifications. This approach occasionally succeeds, but only if the convict possesses some unique skill currently in demand. As a general rule, inmates don't receive the jobs that they request. Consequently, a more savvy convict won't hint at his preference; instead, he misleads the staff member into believing that he would hate being assigned to a work detail that he secretly desires.

The conversation between an experienced convict and an employment officer might sound like this:

OFFICER: Okay, where do you want to work?

INMATE: I worked as a clerk in the library the last time I was here and I got burned. The job was too demanding and I couldn't get enough free time.

OFFICER: So are you saying you don't want a clerk's job?

INMATE: Yeah, I guess so. I don't think I could take working as a clerk anymore. I need something easier—you know, a no-brain job—so I can work on my legal papers and stuff like that.

OFFICER: So where do you want to be assigned?

INMATE: How about the kitchen? That's a pretty simple job and I get to eat real good. I think I'd like to work in the kitchen this time 'round. I got a couple of friends who work in the kitchen who can show me the ropes.

In this example, the inmate does his best to convince the employment officer that he really wants to be assigned to the kitchen detail, which is one of the worst jobs in any prison. The deception includes an explanation of why the inmate prefers this work detail even though he knows that the prison official would consider these as reasons *not* to assign the inmate to the kitchen. (The inmate makes himself seem lazy. Also, having friends who already work in the kitchen suggests a possible conspiracy to smuggle food out.) According to the strategy behind playing the opposites, if the inmate manages to convince the employment officer that he really wants a job in the kitchen, he will be assigned a clerk's job, if one is available.

You would think that the risk of a backfire would limit the use of playing the opposites, but, in fact, the game is popular among inmates. As for those who choose not to play, you can be certain they are careful not to let anyone know their real desires. Prisons seem to reward playing the opposites by punishing honesty.

When I first arrived at Graterford, I questioned the wisdom of this strategy. As a young man, I had been taught to "say what I mean, and mean what I say." More-experienced inmates would often try to explain to me how that philosophy simply doesn't work in prison and that the best way for a prisoner to get what he wanted was to play the opposites. Thoughtful inmates told me that prison staff were trained not to care about inmates' personal preferences and were actually told to make prisoners as uncomfortable as possible. So when a prison administrator discovers an inmate's true preference, this knowledge will be used against him. Others simply said, "Who cares, all you need to know is that it works."

It was difficult for me to accept this conventional wisdom because I believed that corrections staff didn't have time to play petty mind games. I assumed that prison managers would treat inmates impartially. Impartial treatment would consider an individual's likes and dislikes, when balanced with particular job availability and other situational factors. It made no sense to me that staff members would maliciously try to maximize the discomfort of inmates.

Clarence and the Program Review Committee

It was Clarence who convinced me there was more to playing the opposites than mere prison paranoia. Clarence was a drug dealer who had served most of his time and was now awaiting release from Graterford. He was memorable for his razor-sharp wit and pungent sarcasm.

One day, I found myself in a holding room seated next to Clarence, as we waited to speak to the members of the Program Review Committee (PRC) to request a reduction in disciplinary sanctions for infractions we had committed. At the time, anyone who had received a disciplinary sanction could petition the PRC for a reduction of the punishment. The PRC required petitioning inmates to explain why they deserved a reduction in sanctions. Every Thursday, 50 or more inmates would be summoned to the holding room to make a plea for mercy before a panel of three high-ranking prison administrators who called themselves the PRC.

The disciplinary sanction I had received was cell restriction, so I was seated in the waiting room wearing my regular prison uniform. Clarence had been caught trying to smuggle drugs into the institution on a furlough return. Because he had received a disciplinary sanction of six months in the Hole, he was seated next to me in handcuffs, wearing standard dress for the Hole (a prison-stripes jumpsuit).

The PRC always took its time, so someone could expect to wait for hours to plead for mercy. The waiting room was small and unventilated, stuffed with many hot and sweaty men. Waiting in that room was extremely oppressive. I wondered if the PRC had intentionally designed the conditions in the room as a means to discourage men from seeking leniency. Several men left the waiting room in frustration, choosing to abandon their plans to address the PRC rather than to melt.

Clarence was prison-wise and determined to see the process through. He devised a plan to coax more of the men into leaving the room by complaining about the unpleasant conditions. He guessed this would shorten his waiting time.

"Watch this," he said to me, just before he spoke loudly to everyone in the room. "Man, these people must think we're real suckers. They got us all crowded in here sweating and smelling like plantation slaves waiting for their master to give them a neck bone or some other bullshit. Man, fuck the PRC."

This immediately caused some grumbling among the other men, and before long two or three of them left the waiting room. "That makes it a little bit easier to breathe in here," he whispered to me. No doubt, Clarence knew the angles, and that's why I was puzzled by his desire to see the PRC. Certainly, he didn't expect to get a reduction of his time in the Hole, considering the seriousness of his offense.

"What are you here for?" Clarence asked me.

"I'm on cell restriction for stupid stuff. My lock was broken and the guard couldn't unlock it with his key so he wrote me up," I explained.

"That's petty shit! That guard must not like you," he offered.

"I guess not. But tell me, do you really think the PRC is going to cut you any slack?" I asked.

"Sure, sure they will. I bet I get a break before you do!" he eagerly wagered.

"You've got to be kidding! I've got a meatball case and you're in the Hole for smuggling drugs and you think they'll give you a break? You'll be lucky if they don't give you a new street charge!" I scoffed in disbelief.

"Laugh if you want to. But I know how these people work and you don't. See, you'll probably go in there and tell them that you've been a good boy and that the guard was picking on you and that you'll never do it again. Man, they don't want to hear that shit! That's all they hear all day long. You better not tell them that sorry stuff," he warned.

"Yeah, well what do you plan on telling them?" I asked.

"I'm going to get on my hands and knees and beg them, I mean really beg them, to keep me in the damn Hole until they let me go home. That's what I'm going to do," he answered smartly.

"And that's your big plan? You think they'll feel sorry for you and just let you go? Why don't you ask for your drugs back while you're at it?" I asked sarcastically.

"Real funny. I can understand where you're coming from. You think these people care about you. You're really going to be shocked when you find out they don't give a shit about you or me. They couldn't care less about us waiting in this nasty room or you staying locked in your cell 24 hours a day because some guard has a hard-on for you. That's the bottom line. When you understand that, you'll stop doing hard time. See, I know they really want to put a foot up my ass, so when I go in there I'm going to let them do that. I'm going to tell those people that I was bringing the drugs in for a big, mean motherfucker in population and that if they let me out of the Hole, I'm going to get my ass kicked because I can't pay the dude back for the shit that was confiscated. I'm going to beg them not to let me out of the Hole. In fact, I'm going to ask for a transfer," he said with an impressive air of confidence.

"And that's your plan?" I asked.

"Yep, and if I were you, I'd figure out some reason to tell those people why you like it on cell restriction," he suggested.

We spoke together a little longer before the PRC finally escorted Clarence into the hearing room. About 10 or 15 minutes later I saw Clarence being taken back to the Hole. I remember thinking to myself that he was a fool to think that his scheme would work.

Eventually, the PRC called for me and I made my plea. As Clarence had predicted, I explained to the Committee that my infraction was a minor one. I noted that I had a history of good behavior and that I intended to obey all prison rules and regulations in the future. The PRC wasn't impressed and returned me to my cell to serve out the remainder of my restriction. I left the room angry, not for being turned down, but for having spent needless hours suffering in that hot and smelly holding room.

The next day, as I was reading in my cell, I heard a knock on the metal door. I looked up to see Clarence staring down at me. I couldn't believe it. The PRC had released him to the general population. His plan had worked!

"So I see you didn't take my advice," he said with a big grin. I was too stunned to respond. "Maybe this will teach you something about this place. These people don't care nothing about you and the sooner you realize that the better off you'll be." With that, he slowly walked away, whistling like a free man.

Of Rabbits and Inmates

This hasn't been the only incident in my prison experience to convince me that there is merit to playing the opposites, but it certainly was one of the most memorable. I've personally chosen not to play the game; when it comes to expressing my real preferences in prison, I generally remain silent. Still, because I recognize that playing the opposites is an effective tool for getting what you want from prison staff, I've advised inexperienced inmates of its benefits.

If it were simply a "prison thing," playing the opposites wouldn't be of much importance, other than reinforcing stereotypes of inmates as manipulative and dishonest. But the truth is that playing the opposites is an age-old strategy employed by all oppressed people.

I realized this after reading a collection of Uncle Remus stories, tales that were passed down orally by generations of black slaves in America. In one story, Br'er Fox (symbolizing the master) was trying to catch Br'er Rabbit (symbolizing the slave). Br'er Fox fashioned a trap for the rabbit by making a tarbaby (a doll covered with sticky tar) and leaving it out in a field. Br'er Rabbit, thinking the tarbaby was another animal, walked over to talk to it. Gradually, he became ensnared, hopelessly stuck to the doll. The gleeful fox ran out of hiding, gloating about the different ways he might choose to kill the rabbit. Playing along, Br'er Rabbit begged not to be thrown into a nearby brier-patch because, he explained, it would be unbearable to be torn to pieces in the thorns. Naturally, the malicious fox immediately tossed him into the briers. Waiting in the patch were Br'er Rabbit's friends, who freed him from the tarbaby. Hopping away, the clever rabbit ridiculed the fox for being so gullible.

This story reminded me of Clarence in the PRC waiting room. Apparently, playing the opposites is not only an adjustment to prison life but a survival tactic of the disadvantaged everywhere. It is a practice employed by all rabbits, slaves, and inmates to defend themselves against all foxes, masters, and prison staff.

The most troubling aspect of this adjustment is that it encourages deceit as an acceptable means to an end. In prison, it is hard to know when an inmate is being truthful, or when he is playing the opposites. The longer a person remains in prison, the less likely it is that he will be able to share sincere feelings with anyone, a penalty of the ground rules of this game.

Staff are not exempt from the far-reaching effects of these lies. Some officials don't believe anything an inmate says, or they believe the opposite of whatever inmates tell them. In response, some inmates intentionally tell the truth in situations where they know they won't be trusted, perpetuating a cycle of deceit that makes communication almost impossible in prison.

So go the frustrating conversations between foxes and rabbits everywhere, trading an ounce of comic relief in the brier-patch for a pound of distrust, cynicism, and despair in the fields.

Chapter 4

Prison Violence

Editors' Note

Like most modern prisons, Graterford is a violent institution. Although historical data are unavailable, criminologists believe this trend of increasing violence is a recent phenomenon. Its causes are unknown. Some attribute the increase in prison violence to overcrowding per se, though the evidence may not be enough to substantiate this. When American prisons became overcrowded after the end of World War II, for example, the level of violence did not seem to rise in the affected institutions. Other criminologists attribute the trend to one or more specific inadequacies of prisons, ranging from a lack of psychological programs and services to permissive administrators. Finally, like Victor Hassine, there are those who point to changes in the larger society. Prisons have grown more violent, they argue, because society has grown more violent.

This "cultural importation" hypothesis is attractive because of its simplicity, yet it tends to exonerate prison administrators from any blame. Some years ago, Governor Lester Maddox explained the deplorable condition of his state's prisons in this way: "I'll give you better prisons when you give me better prisoners."

Dramatic changes in society sometimes result in equally dramatic changes in prison populations and prison management. When numerous mental hospitals were closed nationwide years ago, releasing thousands of patients into the community, the result was a rapid rise in the imprisonment of the mentally ill, along with the spread of anti-psychotic medications into prisons. Another example is the sudden appearance of AIDS in society and its subsequent devastating impact on the physical health of inmates and on prison medical care. (Hassine discusses both developments in later chapters.)

Still, as a scientific theory, the thesis of cultural importation can be problematic. This is because the importation of particular cultural norms is harder to document.

Rumor had it that Old Man Simpson had been beaten by the KKK as a young man and by white guards in prison. If you were white and walked within arms' reach, Old Man Simpson would punch you in the face without warning. He also had a habit of throwing hot coffee in any white man's face who stood too close to him in the breakfast line. Prison veterans always steered clear, but enjoyed watching him do his thing to newcomers.

But Old Man Simpson's acts of violence were mild compared to the random savagery spread by the new breed of young inmates who swept into the crowded main corridor of Graterford in the 1980s. They threw concentrated cleaning acid or bleach into men's faces, and formed prison gangs that stormed entire cell blocks, slashing prisoners' necks and faces with razor blades.

By 1984, Graterford's population exceeded 2,500. Gangs proliferated at a staggering rate, not only because of high unemployment but because of the need for protection from the gangs' new money-making schemes.

If you couldn't rob a man's cell, you just robbed the man himself. Extortion became very lucrative. One of the favorite ways to deal with a resistant victim was to lock him in his cell and set the cell on fire. So if you were not aligned with a protection gang, it was only a matter of time before you would have to face the "Welcome Wagon" and be challenged to pay or to fight.

The Welcome Wagon visited me shortly after I arrived at Graterford. I was sitting in the movie theater. In those days, prison recreational staff didn't have videotapes, so they showed films in large auditoriums. It gets pretty dark there. I was watching the movie when suddenly I felt this sharp knife on my throat. The guy wasn't asking me for a match! Four or five inmates behind me started talking about how they wanted money and they wanted it quickly. I had the presence of mind to ask them how much they wanted and when, so I could have it dressed up and ready to go. That strategy bought me some time. About two days later, I met the Welcome Wagon again in the yard, but this time I was prepared to fight. After this, they left me alone, preferring easier game.

These were violent and deadly times at Graterford; times of random violence, murders, cell fires, paranoia, and knife carrying. According to the Department of Corrections' Monthly Morbidity Report in 1986-87, Graterford accounted for the highest rate of assaults out of Pennsylvania's 12 state prisons: 392 assaults by inmates against inmates and 47 by inmates against staff, a total of 439.

While it seemed like total anarchy, it really wasn't. This was mob rule with a purpose, a throwback to a time long before civilized man developed modern social institutions. By now I began to realize how fragile civilization was and how easily modern man could be reduced to the savagery of his prehistoric ancestors. Though we had TVs, radios, clothes, and a wealth of commissary goods, behaviorally we had regressed thousands of years backward on the social evolutionary scale. The new order was now the law of the jungle.

Violence in Graterford had also become a form of escape for many inmates. In creating and maintaining a predatory environment, these men were able to avoid the reality of imprisonment by focusing all their attention on fighting one another. The more hostile the environment, the more they saw themselves as victims and the less responsible they felt for their own actions. This obsession with violence became as destructive as any narcotic addiction.

People caught up in this violent escapism never perceived it as their reaction to incarceration, any more than I could see the danger of oversleeping before it was pointed out to me. Sadly, the ones who ended up suffering the most were those who came to prison just to pay their debt to society—those who hoped one day to return to their lives in the mainstream. They suffered twice: once at the hands of the predatory inmates, and then again through the prison's system of punishment.

Prison Subcultures

One of the contributing factors to this upsurge of violence was the creation of new subcultures within the prison. These arose from the new types of inmates who had now extended the roster of victims and predators in the general population. People who in the past would never have been committed to an adult correction facility were now queuing up for their "three hots and a cot" in ever-increasing numbers.

Many of these were the mentally ill who had spilled out of state mental hospitals, which had been closed down in the seventies. These "nuts," as inmates simply called them, were pathetic and destructive. Their illnesses made punishment in the normal sense virtually impossible. Their helplessness often made them the favorite victims of predatory inmates. Worst of all, their special needs and peculiar behavior destroyed the stability of the prison system.

There were also growing numbers of the homeless, as well as juvenile offenders committed as adults. But the largest group of new arrivals were young, minority drug dealers and users, most of them from inner-city ghettos.

When the homeless came to Graterford, they were just looking for a secure haven from the streets. They weren't interested in counselors, treatment, or discipline. They had no sense of their own criminality.

Juveniles suffered the most. They viewed prison as a surrogate parent and so expected to be protected and sheltered. What they got instead was victimization by adult inmates and indifferent bureaucrats.

Finally, the drug addicts and dealers saw Graterford as one more rehab center to dry them up and help them overcome their habit. Few thought of themselves as criminals because they perceived themselves as the victims of their own addictions.

Like me, all these newcomers sought to have their needs met. But Graterford, a maximum-security prison, could not identify these needs, let alone meet them. A prison confines, punishes, and hopefully deters. It is neither designed nor inclined to foster, cure, or rehabilitate.

In meeting only the basic needs of the new arrivals (food, shelter, clothing, and medical care), Graterford's resources were stretched beyond its limits. Additionally, many of the guards and treatment staff, who were accustomed to supplying inmates with only a minimum amount of services and a maximum amount of discipline, were embittered by the fact that these new arrivals were coming into the prison with expectations of receiving treatment and care.

Soon, the mentally ill were commanding too much of the staff's attention. Drug addicts, many of them going through withdrawal, were doing anything they could to get high. Juveniles were being raped and causing havoc trying to attract some "parental" attention. Because of all this, instead of changing people, Graterford itself was changing. Since most of the new commitments came from blighted urban areas, the changes often reflected that environment.

New Inmates vs. Old Heads

Fear and violence had changed Graterford as profoundly as it had changed me. The new prison subcultures with their disrespect for authority, drug addiction, illiteracy, and welfare mentality had altered the institution's very character. All the evils of the decaying American inner city were being compressed into one overcrowded prison. Ironically, the violence which had long been a tool of control by the administration was now being used against it to send its prison system hurtling out of control. Much of the violence that invaded Graterford in the 1980s was actually imported from the streets by the social misfits who were now being called convicts. They were criminals before—the only change in their identity is that now they're incarcerated. For many of these newcomers, prison violence was simply life as usual.

Reacting to this new environment, the Old Heads would tell anyone who would listen about the "good old days." The typical Old Head had come to Graterford a decade or more earlier after spending most of his life behind bars. What puzzled me and others my age was how these seasoned prison elders would pine over the rigidly structured routine, solitude, mistreatment, and hard labor of those good old days. When asked about it, they would talk about times when the outside world was kept outside, when an inmate's natural enemies were the guards, and when men did extraordinary things to go home.

Now those good old days had become a bygone era. To the Old Heads, prison life today lacked the honor, quiet solitude, and routine that had once made incarceration more noble. Now the greatest threat to an inmate had become other inmates, particularly the "young bucks" who had infested the general population.

An example of this new threat was the way debts were collected. Old Heads were always careful to whom they gave credit. If a debtor fell behind in payments, the debt was usually doubled and any of his belongings would be taken as collateral. Physical violence was employed only as a last resort.

In contrast, the young bucks would lend anything to anybody. Should a debtor be late in paying, even if it was a single pack of cigarettes, he would immediately be beaten and robbed. It seemed almost as if these compulsive youths were more interested in committing violence than in making money. This all too common practice of swift punishment for indebtedness disturbed the Old Heads' sense of fair play. "Working from the muscle" was to them unsound business, but the young bucks would have it no other way. To the Old Heads nothing in business was personal, but to the young newcomers *everything* was personal.

What disturbed the Old Heads most was how these newcomers had so readily and completely accepted prison as their life. Everything they did, including using and dealing drugs, smuggling contraband, forming violent gangs, and embracing homosexuality, was undertaken to make themselves more comfortable *in* prison—not to get *out* of prison. Few of them challenged their convictions in court and still fewer contemplated escape. They were too busy enjoying themselves.

This confounded the Old Heads, who could not conceive of a life beyond the walls so oppressive that it would cause all these strong and able-bodied young men to forfeit their freedom so willingly. Nor could the Old Heads win in their losing battle against the new prison subculture of young bucks who fought for prison turf as if it were their birthright.

To illustrate this conflict between generations, one of my closest Old Head friends was released from prison the day after he had slapped a young buck in the prison yard because "he didn't know how to talk to a man." Some time after his release, my friend was shot to death in a bar by that same young man, who had recklessly sought revenge beyond the prison walls with no regard for the consequences. The assassin has since been caught and now sits on death row.

The Meat Wagon Crew

By 1984, years after I had lost my clerical job, I was working as an infirmary janitor. Stabbings, murders, and serious injuries had become so frequent that the medical staff created a special unit, to which I was assigned. Our job was to respond to the medical emergencies on the general population blocks.

They called us the "Meat Wagon Crew." When summoned, we would rush to the scene of a medical emergency, a staff nurse in the lead, one inmate pushing a gurney, another carrying an emergency medical kit, and a third bearing oxygen or medical equipment. While our crew was originally intended to serve as an ambulance service, it in fact more closely resembled a coroner's wagon. Two or three times a week, we could be seen rushing through the many long concrete corridors in response to an emergency call. Often we arrived only in time to remove a dead body or the unconscious victim of an assault.

In one case, an inmate had died of a drug overdose. He sat frozen on his bed, his lifeless eyes still staring out of a window. Inattentive guards simply added him to their usual count, while passing inmates wondered what could be so interesting outside. Finally, someone asked the stiff body that question, only to discover that dead men don't talk. When the Meat Wagon arrived, we had to struggle to get the rigid corpse out of the cell's narrow opening to the waiting gurney.

In most cases, if the medical emergency didn't involve a drug overdose, it was usually some aftermath of violence. One inmate, who had been attacked over nonpayment of a two-cigarette-pack debt, was found with his intestines spilling out from a razor slash across his stomach. We had to keep pushing his entrails back into place as we raced the gurney down the corridor. Another man's face had been so badly beaten that I didn't recognize him as one of my friends until a guard identified him from his I.D. card.

By 1985, the body count was so high that we stopped running to answer our calls. The helpless victimization of our fellow inmates and our own frustration eventually rendered us indifferent to violence.

Violence or degradation, self-defense or lost self-esteem, kill or be killed—these are not real choices. In the same way, Graterford offered no real choices to the multitude of men overcrowded within its walls. The violence of inmates was no worse than the brutality and insensitivity of an indifferent, omnipotent bureaucracy. In the long run Graterford's great walls would never be high enough to contain the hatred, violence, and rage swelling out of proportion inside.

Chapter 5

The Underground Economy

Editors' Note

The underground economy that the author describes in this chapter is a complex adaptive system. At the highest level, the system balances the supply and demand of goods and services. At the lowest level, it rewards and punishes the behavior of individuals. At intermediate levels, it responds in arcane ways to minor changes in the environment, especially changes in the "official" economy. When shortages appear in the official economy, the underground economy steps up production to fill the void. It assures inmates an uninterrupted supply of necessary goods and services, though at a cost. Although all inmates benefit from this underground economy to some extent, benefits are not distributed equally.

The underground economy also creates expectations among its component members, forming the basis of an underground society—a "Kingdom of Inmates" in this case—that is reflected in the spontaneous cooperative actions described in this chapter. Readers may wonder why, if the prison administration does not benefit from this underground economy, it allows it to exist. There is no simple answer to this question.

Drug dealers in prison often use homosexuals to smuggle contraband. For this reason, some homosexuals in prison enlarge their anal cavities so they can hide drugs in greater quantities. Since many prison "mules" work on a percentage basis, larger cavities translate into more money. Mules are sometimes even paid to carry contraband in their cavities all day long. They become walking safe-deposit boxes.

By the mid-1980s, Graterford was in the advanced stages of a complete system breakdown. Not only had the prison become an extremely violent place, but the administration was showing signs of an inability to meet the inmate population's basic need for food and shelter. This breakdown, however, opened the door for a thriving underground economy which provided virtually every kind of goods and services that the legitimate prison system now lacked.

For example, if I wanted my laundry done, I could pay an inmate laundry worker with cigarettes to have my laundry picked up, cleaned, and delivered back to me. If, on the other hand, I had tried to send my laundry through the institution's authorized laundry system, I probably would never have gotten it back. Thieves and hustlers who profited from the underground laundry made sure that the prison laundry was unable to meet the population's needs. So for two or three 50-cent packs a week, an inmate could get his laundry cleaned and returned, which was a real bargain. Those who had no cigarettes wore dirty clothes or washed their own laundry.

Other black-market services abounded at Graterford, especially in the main corridor where most business was conducted. For a few packs a week, a swag man could deliver specialized cooked foods and pastries to your cell on a daily basis. The food was smuggled out of the kitchen by inmate workers who would then openly hawk them on any housing block. These swag men were the most prolific of the underground service providers and, since the food cost them nothing, also the best paid. The quality of bootlegged sandwiches was comparable to or better than that of the food served in the dining hall. But this said more about the breakdown of Graterford's food service than about the culinary skills of the swag men.

Eventually, I worked my way into a situation where my own basic needs were being met. I had at my disposal the eager services of swag men, laundry men, ice men (for summer ice cubes), barbers (to cut my hair in my cell), and phone men (to make sure I got signed up for phone calls). I could even have a cell cleaner, though I felt there were certain things a man should do for himself.

All in all, Graterford had become a predatory institution where nothing worked right and everything was for sale.

A Kingdom of Tribal Gangs

Through this gradual process of deterioration, Graterford the prison became Graterford the ghetto: a place where men forgot about courts of law or the differences between right and wrong because they were too busy thinking about living, dying, or worse.

Reform, rehabilitation, and redemption do not exist in a ghetto. There is only survival of the fittest. Crime, punishment, and accountability are of little significance when men are living in a lawless society where their actions are restrained only by the presence of concrete and steel walls. Where a prison in any real or abstract sense might promote the greater good, once it becomes a ghetto it can do nothing but promise violent upheaval.

As weapons in Graterford proliferated, violence escalated, and gang leadership emerged; the administration gradually ceded control of the institution to independent gang tribes. During this period of gang expansion, there was no method to the madness. Violence was as unpredictable as the weather. By 1986, it was still epidemic, but it had more direction. Most of the violence was now directed at people who failed to pay their debts. The underground economy was so healthy at this point that it needed to take further steps in order to defend and preserve its fiscal survival.

Double D and Rocky

It is hard to find friends in prison, because most inmates are anti-social by disposition or through conditioning. One of the cruelest aspects of a penitentiary is the way it leaves one isolated and lonely despite the overcrowded surroundings. Yet, because of all the fear and hardship we experienced together, the friends I made at

Graterford turned out to be my closest. The harsher the conditions, the closer the bonds between us.

Dan, my chess companion and one of my earliest friends at Graterford, was a quiet, soft-spoken man who stood a tall six feet and weighed about 180 pounds. His prison handle was Double D, an abbreviation for Dangerous Dan.

I had met Double D when I was in the county jail awaiting trial. For some reason he took a liking to me. I would prefer to think it was because of my dynamic personality, charm, and wit, but in prison such qualities don't account for much. Chances are, he liked me because he felt I was of some use to him. I've never really been certain why but, whatever the reason, I valued his friendship highly in those early years.

Dan never talked much, didn't lie, didn't steal, and didn't mince words. Though he belonged to no prison gang, he was respected by everyone. Those who didn't respect him feared him to the very marrow of their bones.

We both loved chess and, while he was a much better opponent, I played well enough for him to enjoy beating me. We played a lot on the block, because I didn't like being too far away from my cell. The good thing about chess is that it's not a spectator sport and is so boring to watch that it kept people away. Dan and I were able to have long, leisurely games and conversations without distraction.

"Why do they call you 'Dangerous?'" I once asked.

"Because they know I won't take any shit from any of these fleas."

"A lot of guys are afraid of you."

Dan rubbed his forehead and pushed up the brim of his ever-present prison work cap. Its tightly creased brim stood at a crisp 45 degrees to the ceiling, moving around like the dorsal fin of a shark. After a long silence, he replied, "I like it like that."

I must confess that being a friend of Double D's had certain advantages. One was the freedom to play chess without ever having to worry about an ambush or an attack, fairly common events in those days.

Once while we were playing, a mountain of a brute walked by. Dan never looked up, but I could sense he was watching the man's every move. I could also sense there was no love lost between them.

Rocky was the biggest and toughest convict in Graterford, and inmates and staff alike paid deference to him. He led a gang of black and white thugs called the "Terminators," which he liked to refer to as a paramilitary organization of anti-government terrorists. I had been told that Rocky's Terminators were the largest gang of extortionists, drug dealers, and smugglers in the prison. But to Double D, "Rocky's just another flea."

"You don't like him?" I asked one day after I made a rather stupid chess move.

"No. Pay attention to the board," Dan said in that soft voice.

"Why do you think they let him do the shit he does?"

Dan gritted his teeth with annoyance and rubbed his forehead, the shark fin of his cap circling the air. "Because he works for the prison. He's doing exactly what they want him to."

I had played enough chess with Double D to know his words were as complicated as his chess strategy.

"What do you mean?"

The fin came toward me. "This place only lets happen what it wants to happen. Rocky's no bigger than the 300 guards they got working here. That silly Terminator stuff is just bullshit. They use Rocky to keep everybody in line. He does their dirty work." Then he proceeded to beat me mercilessly on the chessboard, as if to emphasize his point.

According to Double D, Graterford had gone through some violent changes in the 1970s. Despite its rigidity and strict military discipline, three staff members had been murdered. One was a captain of the guard who in 1979 had had his head split open by a baseball bat in the main corridor. By the early 1980s, prison gangs had become firmly entrenched and the administration did not have the manpower or the know-how to deal with them. Furthermore, the rigidity and discipline did nothing to make their jobs any easier.

So, as Dan saw it, the administration decided to play a gambit: they relaxed the rules and, instead of trying to end the gangs, they manipulated them by playing one against the other. In this way gangs would be too busy fighting each other to work together against the system. To destabilize these gangs, the administration threw its support behind one gang to maintain a balance of power. So Rocky's Terminators became the administration's flavor of the month.

To me, this seemed too far-fetched to be the product of any rational administrative policy. Besides, it sounded illegal; you can't support corruption if you're paid to combat it. But in those days I knew very little about the prison system. So I discounted Double D's story, reasoning that the Terminators' success was more likely due to administrative ineptitude. The staff was simply as frightened of Rocky as were most of the inmates.

"Rocky's going to get himself killed," volunteered Double D one day, as he murdered me on the chess board.

"Why do you say that?" I asked, knocking my king over.

"Because people are getting tired of his bullshit. The administration can't protect him forever."

The conversation ended there. I couldn't imagine a thug like Rocky needing protection from anyone.

About a year later, gang wars broke out and numerous inmates were getting stabbed. Double D and I still played chess together regularly, but we were a lot more wary.

One day a friend of Dan's, Shorty, got beat up by Rocky over a phone call. Rocky wanted to use a phone Shorty was on, so he just picked up the little guy and threw him to the ground like a rag. Shorty was no coward, but Rocky was twice his size. It was a no-win situation.

Later that same day, Double D took the time to warn me: "Don't come out in the main corridor when they open up tonight. Just stay on the block."

But I was too young and curious, unable to imagine that the main corridor could be any more dangerous than it already was. When the evening bell rang, I locked my cell and ventured out, staying close to the guard's station just to play it safe. All seemed normal, except the traffic was extremely light. Too light for a prison of over 2,000 men. The main corridor exhibited a dreary glow, like the light of a fading fluorescent lamp.

Suddenly, the corridor became completely empty. A deadly silence gripped the scene. Some feet away, a guard ordered me back to my block as he scanned the corridor in puzzlement. Usually there would be last-minute stragglers loitering about, but now there was not a soul in sight.

As I started for B-Block, I felt a slight breeze. I looked up the corridor to see the auditorium door angled open—inmates were spilling out into the corridor. I was too far away to make out details, but I could tell that a huge mob was quietly filling the back end of the corridor and heading in my direction. It was an eerie, unsettling sight to see hundreds of men rush down a long corridor in utter silence.

Rocky happened to be coming out of the door directly to my right. When he saw the approaching mob, he ran as fast as a man his size could toward A-Block. He banged on the gate, yelling, "Key up! Key up!"

When the mob saw this, they all bolted in unison down the corridor toward him, shouting angrily.

The guard on A-Block, instead of retreating to the safety of the guards' station, courageously rushed to Rocky's aid, keyed the convict into his block, and locked the door behind him. Then in some fit of insanity he stood in the center of the corridor, raised his hand, and hollered, "Everybody back to your blocks! That's an order!" But the unstoppable mob ran over him on their way to confront Rocky and his Terminators.

Some men banged on the door to A-Block and screamed, "Key! Key!" Amazingly enough, another guard opened it and let through a stream of men before he realized his folly and slammed the door shut. The rest of the crowd streamed through the door from which Rocky had emerged moments earlier.

Leading the pack were Double D and Shorty. When he saw me watching in amazement from the corridor, Dan waved me away. His mob then disappeared into the dark doorway until all of them had emptied out of the main corridor. All that was left were me and the trampled guard still lying on the floor. Quickly guards hurried out of their station to drag their co-worker to safety. I myself rushed to the B-Block door and was lucky enough to be let in.

Soon the mob returned to occupy the corridor, hollering in triumph. This wasn't the Battle of Lexington or the Boston Tea Party, but the consequences were just as profound for Graterford.

No one was killed in this bloodless coup, but things changed rapidly. Rocky, the Terminator's leader, was transferred out of the prison that night. The next day, a number of his gang members were stabbed in separate incidents. Many of the others took self-lockup.

From that day forward, no one gang dominated at Graterford. If Double D's story was true, then the administration had lost its balance of power. Soon whole gangs of cell thieves were being stabbed and beaten. Just as these gangs had once made the administration superfluous, the collective will of the inmate population had now made the gangs superfluous.

Hence, the "Kingdom of Inmates" was born. Its new offensive curtailed much of the stealing which the administration had been unable to control. A collective conscience had risen among the inmates, as Graterford evolved from a ragtag nation of independent tribal gangs into a unified conglomerate of collective and competing interests. It was only a matter of time before the new kingdom would begin to test its boundaries by challenging the power of the prison administration.

The Inmate Code of Conduct

In retrospect, it was primarily the inability of Graterford's guards to ensure inmates' safety that brought about the demise of their control over their own prison. When things got so bad that inmates couldn't even commit themselves to protective custody, the population knew it had to fend for itself. The only thing guards could do for inmates now was to keep them locked in their cells.

Because of this, the population developed its own unwritten "Inmate Code of Conduct," which stood apart from the prison administration's rules and regulations. The Code went something like this: "Don't gamble, don't mess with drugs, don't mess with homosexuals, don't steal, don't borrow or lend, and you might survive."

By itself, this simple rule would never have worked unless something tangible and powerful prevented the inmates from killing each other and forced them to abide by it. That something was the flourishing underground economy. The black market of goods and services had grown so much as a result of overcrowding and failed security that a stable class of merchants and consumers had established itself within the prison population.

The swag man who sold me and others his sandwiches became my friend. But if it hadn't been so easy and profitable to steal from the kitchen, he probably would have ended up stealing from me. The more he provided his clandestine services, the more he created a demand, which in turn ensured him a steady income that was far less risky than breaking into another man's cell.

Every inmate in general population was either a buyer or a seller. It was now to everyone's benefit to abide by the Inmate Code of Conduct, so that the economic heart of the Inmate Kingdom could continue to beat.

The only threat to this economic stability, then, became the guards. Since they were no longer the mainstays of stability or providers of protection, their petty rules, shake-downs, and confiscations served only as an irritating nuisance that hindered the inmate population's new economic order. The Kingdom of Inmates had no choice but to challenge the authority of the guards in order to discourage their interference with the socio-economic balance.

Chicken Sunday

It is difficult to determine exactly when Graterford's guards yielded their authority to their charges, but one significant turning point took place on Super Bowl Sunday of 1983. An inmate left the C-Block dining room and headed for his cell, openly carrying a paper plate piled high with the usual Sunday chicken dinner and all its trimmings. It was his intention not to let his favorite meal interfere with his watching the Super Bowl on the TV in his cell. Posted everywhere around him were signs dictating, "NO FOOD IS TO LEAVE THE DINING ROOM."

While violations of this rule were commonplace, the usual practice was to hide one's food before leaving the dining hall. To accommodate this minimal demand for obedience, most inmates smuggled out food in anything from trash-bag liners to empty potato-chip bags, often stashed in the split lining of one's institutional prison coat. Guards never searched for food, and no harm was done.

But on this particular day, this inmate had decided to blatantly ignore convention. As was expected, a guard saw him with the food plate, followed him to his cell, and ordered him either to eat his food in the dining hall or throw it out. Considering the circumstances, this was a reasonable request.

The inmate told the guard in no uncertain terms that he planned to eat his Super Bowl meal in the comfort of his cell and there was nothing he could do about it. The guard, frustrated by this display of disrespect, grabbed the plate of food out of the man's hands.

What ensued became known as the Super Bowl Sunday Chicken Riot. Since C-Block housed many winemakers and this was a big sports day, a good number of the block's 400 occupants were drunk on "pruno," or prison hootch. When they saw this inmate's fight with the guard, everybody decided it was time to show the staff who was boss. Every inmate related to the incident as if the guard had tried to take away something of *his*. The chicken was more than just food—it represented each man's hustle, and its confiscation challenged everyone's livelihood.

Dozens of men swarmed to the aid of the inmate and beat the guard. Dozens more mobbed the dining room to defiantly take chicken dinners back to their cells. In quick order, every guard on the block was assaulted and some were even locked in cells.

Notably, the inmates attacked only guards and not each other. Not a single inmate was hurt in the uprising, which made this event uniquely different from other prison riots. If anything, the inmates actually joined together with a coherent plan. Some seized a guard's radio transmitter and called for reinforcements, while others armed with sticks and clubs waited in ambush by the block's main entrance. When a dozen or so guards rushed into the block, inmates fell upon them like swashbuckling pirates and quickly subdued them. Then they locked their new victims into cells.

What happened next was the most convincing proof that a kingdom had arisen. The inmates abused and humiliated the guards—but they didn't seriously injure any of them. Once they were satisfied, they simply opened the main door to C-block and allowed other guards to tend to their fallen comrades, just so they could see what might one day await them. Some inmates even assisted the nursing staff in tending to the wounds of guards they had attacked only moments before. There were no demands for better conditions, amnesty, media, the superintendent, or anything else.

And that was the end of the Super Bowl Sunday Chicken Riot. Most of the inmates simply returned to their cells to watch the Super Bowl Game, drink jailhouse wine, and eat chicken. Nothing else happened for the rest of the day. At the 5:00 p.m. count, everyone locked up in their cells as usual. It wasn't until then that guards quietly gathered the rebellious inmates from their cells and escorted them to the Hole.

By then it was too late. The point had been made. Inmates had joined together to defeat the guards fair and square. The interests of the inmate population had been advanced and defended, thus ensuring the livelihood of each and every man in the triumphant Kingdom of Inmates.

To this day, Graterford is still the most violent prison in the state system. It now houses over 4,000 men and is home to the most politically active inmate population in Pennsylvania. If you ask any staff member or inmate who runs Graterford, the answer will always be the same: "The inmates run Graterford."

Chapter 6

Prison Politics

Editors' Note

In this chapter, Hassine describes how a prison's political system operates on a day-to-day basis. Unlike the underground economy, which thrives on change, the political system opposes change of any sort. While the staff is generally not allowed to participate in the underground economy, some (though not all) of them are willing participants in the prison's political system.

From the author's perspective, inmates and staff who have this political participation in common tend to benefit from the status quo. By resisting change, the political system maintains the status quo and ensures that those few who are on top today stay on top tomorrow. The main differences between participating inmates and guards are the methods each uses to maintain this status quo. As described by the author, a prison's political system does not seem much different from political systems everywhere.

"Put your trust in the Lord; your ass belongs to me!"

—Warden Norton, addressing new inmates
The Shawshank Redemption
Castle Rock Entertainment, 1994

The balance of power has changed much in prisons since the 1950s, when real superintendents like the fictional Warden Norton often made this infamous boast. The process of change within the prison system can be as treacherous as the most notorious of its inhabitants. The danger associated with navigating the murky waters of jailhouse politics makes that change sometimes very difficult to control.

Change in society is inevitable, but in prison there are powerful competing groups of differing interests with much time on their hands and a strong motivation to prevent change. A prison's very existence often depends on the struggles to control change. Its soul is not reflected by the preciseness of its construction nor the orderly appearance of its uniformed staff. Nor does the calculated chaos and deliberately random violence of its inmates necessarily expose the real belly of the beast. Only on the battlefield of resistance to change will one be likely to find the naked prison as it exists.

Much like soldiers in combat, inmates and prison staff have little overview of the arena where their conflicts play out. They can only glean narrow glimpses of it from the small plots of turf they happen to occupy at any given moment. Consequently, inmates and guards alike can never afford themselves a complete view of the prison in which they live, work, and struggle.

In any prison system, the parties of competing interests are represented by the inmate population, the rank-and-file uniformed staff, and the managerial administration. The interaction among these three groups defines a prison at any given time. Those few times when all three parties are in agreement over some particular change, the result is a quick and effective implementation of that change. Likewise, when all three parties are completely united in their opposition to an impending change, the result is unanimous rejection, even though other unrelated and unexpected changes might occur because of competitive tactics employed by one or more of them to resist the original change.

By far the most common and most volatile type of change in a modern prison comes as the result of two groups attempting to impose change over the objections and resistance of the third group. Even though the decision of the majority will be upheld, the resisting minority will nevertheless be relentless in its attempt to undermine that change. The end result is most often some dysfunctional change where conditions are worsened by the minority's resistance. Thus, the intended change is never fully realized. Reluctant change is always more destructive, because jailhouse politics tends to maintain and perpetuate any ongoing struggle.

The Sergeant, the Major, and Me

One illustration of the complexity of prison politics was revealed to me soon after my ill-fated hamburger caper in 1981. There was an unexpected consequence to that infraction of which I was not initially aware.

After my misconduct hearing, I returned to my cell to begin serving my 60 days of cell restriction. At the time, I genuinely felt I was being mistreated. Compared to the rampant thievery and abundance of violence I had witnessed in Graterford, my measly infraction was hardly worth the bother. Losing my job and paying for the burgers made sense, but two months locked in my cell for 22 hours a day seemed unfair to me.

Little did I realize that there were higher forces who felt I had been treated too leniently and who wanted to thrust me into the lions' den of jailhouse politics. In actual fact, stealing food from a penitentiary kitchen was a serious offense because it involved two vital concerns of the administration: spending and control. Graterford spent an average of $2.75 per day to feed a single inmate, in contrast to the statewide average of about $2.10 per day. To the powers that be, the ease with which I was able to buy smuggled food from the kitchen meant that the prison could not control its inmates. If other inmates similarly challenged its control, the per diem cost of feeding the population could rise drastically.

Ten pounds of bootlegged ground beef should have landed me directly in the Hole. The fact that I used the Major of the Guards' bathroom in my plot normally should also have cost me double time in cold storage for my arrogant defiance of authority. If anything, cell restriction was a lucky break for me. But what did I know? I hadn't been in prison long enough to appreciate the seriousness of the situation.

When I finally arrived at my cell, I was unexpectedly greeted by the B-Block Sergeant. A man of military bearing, he stood a rigid six-feet tall in a starched and precisely creased uniform. His prison dress cap added height to his authority.

"Didn't think I'd be seeing you back so soon," the Sergeant said, chewing on a lump of tobacco in his cheek that gave his southern drawl a lazier tone. He spat to accentuate his words.

I assumed he was referring to my returning so soon from the misconduct hearing. Usually men given cell restriction took their time coming back in an effort to extend their liberties.

"I got 60 days cell restriction, Sarge," I complained naively. "Can you believe that?"

The Sergeant spat again. "Boy, the way I see it, you must be a real important inmate to have talked your way out of the Hole. I don't like important inmates on my block, so you just watch yourself because you can be right sure I'll be watching you."

With that, he double-locked me in and walked away like a general who had just reviewed his troops. Amazed by his hostility, I foolishly thought he was singling me out for some personal reason, perhaps because I was Jewish.

However, the truth was that the Sergeant's attitude had nothing to do with me but with my former work supervisor, the Major of the Guard, who had intervened on my behalf to keep me out of the Hole. This recently appointed officer happened to be the only African American in Pennsylvania history to hold such a position. As such, he was the first member of a minority to personally direct the actions of an historically all-white guard force at Graterford. Additionally, he had been promoted from the rank of Lieutenant, which was not only unprecedented but caused a stir among the several Captains he was promoted over.

To further complicate the situation, the Major was also a reformer, a compassionate and decent man who did not feel that physical force was the way to solve Graterford's problems. In his view, such a traditional style of prison management often led to the unfair treatment that had thrust Graterford into a crisis in the first place.

While the prison administration and the overwhelmingly African-American inmate population were hopeful about the Major, the almost all-white, rank-and-file staff were disgruntled over his appointment. Not only had a longstanding race barrier been broken, but there was genuine concern that the Major's management style would give the prison away to the inmates. Militarism and white leadership had been the way at Graterford for generations.

When the Major had decided that my actions were not serious enough to warrant sending me to the Hole, battle lines were drawn. Derogatory slurs were already being made about him by the uniformed staff, often in the presence of inmates, which only served to undermine the Major's authority.

There I was in the middle of all this, and I didn't even know it. I simply wasn't yet tuned in to the political undercurrents sweeping through Graterford.

While on cell restriction, I was let out of my cell for two hours each day for recreation. During this time, I found myself and my cell constantly being searched by the block guards. Though they were not as intrusive as they could have been, even one search of a man's cell or body is an assault on his sense of dignity and freedom.

Naturally, my resentment and paranoia grew with each search, as if every guard was out to get me. Helpless to stop them, I began to hate these men in uniform. To make matters worse, some of them would ridicule and taunt me by calling me the "Major's boy." At times they would even imply that I had avoided the Hole by being a snitch. The mere suggestion of such a label in a prison like Graterford was life-threatening.

On the 59th day of my 60 days of cell restriction, I was issued another misconduct—for taking more than two hours for recreation. Reporting to another misconduct hearing, I was given an additional 30 days of cell restriction. As I returned to my cell, the Sergeant was again waiting for me.

He spat a wad. "Boy, I don't know why you came back to this block. You got no job and you just keep breaking the rules." He spat again. "You must know some real important people. But let me tell you this. Let any of my officers catch you wrong again and nobody's going to be able to save you then."

This time I said nothing, though I'm certain the hatred beating in my heart could be heard by the Sergeant as he locked me in and paraded out of sight. For all my frustration and anger, I was too young and inexperienced to realize that his malice was focused elsewhere. The old soldier was just trying to stop the process of change. His real enemy was the black Major with his liberal notions. I was just someone who was unlucky enough to be chosen as the vehicle for his resentment.

Resistance to change in a prison can foment enough resentment and malice to result in changes so riddled with compromise that more problems are created than solved. The only beneficiaries of this kind of change are those who will profit from the system's breakdown. As a 17-year veteran of jailhouse politics, I can now only speculate what could have transpired had the Sergeant approved of the Major. Could Graterford have become a better place? No one will ever know.

The Politics of Anger

I always considered myself a proud American and, despite my incarceration, I still subscribe to the traditional American system of values. Before coming to prison, I expected it to be a very unpleasant place, staffed by the otherwise unemployable and inhabited by the generally unredeemable. While I was not surprised by the amount of violence and corruption at Graterford, I was genuinely shocked by the level of persecution.

The Sergeant did much to shape my current reality. He accomplished this by continuing to have the block guards pat me down and search my cell, even after I had completed all my cell-restriction time. Generally, this type of treatment was reserved for troublemakers and drug dealers. I was neither. Though the searches never turned up anything of consequence, my cell was always left in total disarray. My creature comforts, such as an extra pillow, bed sheet, and towel, were taken away from me.

Beyond the unfair treatment, the Sergeant had succeeded in making me feel even more isolated from the world that existed outside the prison walls. I was no longer so proud to be an American. I was just a convict without rights. But again, I had simply misconstrued the motives behind his actions.

When prison guards feel they are losing control, their first response is to crack down hardest on the segment of the population over whom they still have control. This is done as a show of force to let the general population know that they mean business. Furthermore, if cooperative inmates are being treated this harshly, then the troublesome ones can expect much more serious treatment.

The problem with this control tactic is that it doesn't always work. Often the uncooperative elements of the population don't necessarily get the message or don't care about the consequences of their actions. When this happens, conditions usually worsen. There is still a control problem, only now it exists with the added hostility and resentment of the more stable inmates.

I was now made to feel the full weight of forced confinement in an imposed egalitarian police state. All my life I had been taught to work for my livelihood; the harder I worked and the more resourceful I was, the greater would be my reward. But now everything was turned around. No matter how hard I worked, or even if I worked at all, I received the same portion as everyone else. There was no incentive to achieve anything or improve myself. In fact, the more well-behaved I was, the more likely it was that I would be mistreated by inmates and staff.

Prison anger affects every aspect of prison life and management. At Graterford it made victims of the Major, the Sergeant, and me. We were all left wondering what kind of world we had fashioned and, each in our own way, resented having to live in it. While anger usually demands satisfaction, it often settles just for company. I had now resolved that the inmate population would be my new nation. And the first thing I would do was join the Graterford Lifers Organization.

Omar and the Lifers Group

"I need a pass for the Lifers meeting," I told the guard seated at a small, shabby desk in the middle of the B-Block "Bridge." The Bridge was a ten-foot walkway that spanned the two upper-tier walkways of the block like the center crossline of a big "H." Behind me stood 20 other men waiting for their passes off the block. I spent a good deal of my time at Graterford waiting in one line or another.

"I didn't know you were a lifer," replied the weary, disaffected bridge officer, a phone receiver cradled between his shoulder and ear. Routine had just about made him a part of the furniture he was stuck in. His hands quickly fingered my inmate I.D. card, but he never looked up. He knew me only from the identity photo.

Without answering, I silently waited for my pass. He slid back to me a standardized slip of paper and my I.D. card. I took both immediately and headed down to the ground floor of B-Block.

Once I reached the block's main entrance, I waited my turn in yet another line, this time for the front-door officer to allow me off the block.

"I didn't know you were a lifer," the door guard said, echoing the bridge officer.

Again I waited silently until he decided to verify my pass. I then entered the main corridor and merged with a moving mass of inmates. During general movement, hundreds of men walked quickly up and down the corridor. Most of them wore prison uniforms for work or exercise clothes for the yard, but there were always some in pajamas and bathrobes whose only apparent purpose was to be part of the confusion.

As I headed for the auditorium, I could hear the familiar voices of hustlers hawking sandwiches, drugs, and anything else worth selling. Hundreds of voices bounced off the concrete walls, the usual disconcerting din which always heightened my concern that I might accidentally collide with the wrong guy. Sometimes the carnival atmosphere here made me forget the dangers of this place. But invariably, I would witness the all too common corridor knifing and be reminded once again how risky it was to commute on this prison's main boulevard.

Halfway to E-Block, I arrived at the main entrance of the auditorium, one of its four doors wedged open with a guard blocking the way inside. I gave him my pass, which he glanced at and quickly returned without a word. All his attention was focused on the many shadows speeding past him in both directions. There were no other guards in sight, so his safety was more of a priority than my status as a lifer. Besides, who would attend a Lifers meeting if he wasn't a lifer?

Crumpling the pass and tossing it, I stepped inside into a dusky twilight. The auditorium, used on weekends as a movie theater, had its lights dimmed down to ambush dark. This would explain why the door guard chose to take his chances in the more brightly lit corridor.

A few feet inside, I was greeted by the first row of steel-framed theater chairs. The auditorium could seat about 1,000 men in three descending columns of these battered folding seats. Deep within was a flat area of space flanked by two basketball hoops mounted on the wall. Directly adjacent to this was an elevated stage that stood a few feet off the floor. It had a large, dirty white projection screen pulled down in front of it.

As I looked down at the farthest row of seats, I could see about a hundred indistinguishable figures either standing, sitting, or slouching. Three men stood alone together, facing the audience.

I couldn't make out anybody I knew well enough to sit next to, so I just walked down to the third row and took an aisle seat. Soon after, I heard the sound of a heavy steel door slam and lock. Shut in from the noisy corridor, I was unaccustomed to such eerie quiet.

"I call this meeting to order," said the tallest of the three standing men.

I had never been to a Lifers meeting and I wasn't sure I wanted to be there now to listen to some of Pennsylvania's most vicious killers. But since I'd become one of the boys, I decided it was time to meet my fellow lifers. Besides, I longed to be a part of a self-governing body.

There were three inmate social organizations in Graterford at the time: the Lifers' Organization, the Knights of Henry Christof, and the Jaycees [Junior Chamber of Commerce]. Each of them was allowed to raise funds in the prison through the sale of food or by providing services, such as showing movies and taking photos in the visiting room. Prison gangs would inevitably dominate these groups and try to control or manipulate any money-making ventures that they undertook.

As the tall man spoke, everyone appeared attentive. The meeting followed a reasonable order of business, with questions asked and politely answered. I soon felt so completely at ease that I wanted to join the discussion in some way.

The tall man gave the floor to the shortest man, apparently the financial officer, who started giving a business report. I knew the lifers sold soda and potato chips to the population on weekends during the auditorium movies. What I didn't know was that they were allowed to make profits and maintain a bank account. I was thrilled to hear that a private enterprise zone actually existed in Graterford. Maybe a little too thrilled.

When the speaker concluded his report, I enthusiastically stood up and asked a question. "Excuse me, I heard you say we have money in a bank account. I just wondered, how much do we have on deposit and how much revenue do we generate?"

I don't know why I stood up but, from the sudden focus of attention on me and the mumbling around me, I realized that standing up in a Lifers meeting meant a lot more than I had intended. Things got ugly real quick.

"Why do you want to know?" asked the speaker.

"Well, I just wondered how much money we were making," I replied a little defensively.

"What are you, a troublemaker?"

"What are you talking about? I asked a simple question and I'd like an answer." Instinct had trained me not to let anyone talk down to me.

It was obvious I had hit a nerve. The prudent thing would have been to sit down quietly and forget the whole matter. But prudence in Graterford was seldom a viable option since it was often mistaken for weakness.

"Why don't you sit down and dig yourself," said the tall speaker.

At this point I felt a tugging at my shirt sleeve. An older man in his mid-forties materialized in the seat beside mine, smiling up at me. As my focus was on the escalating trouble in front of me, I just pulled my arm away and answered the speaker.

"I'll sit down when I get an answer."

The tall man took a step toward me, and I turned toward the aisle to confront him. Once again I felt that tugging at my sleeve and glanced over at the widening smile of my neighbor.

The short speaker reclaimed my attention. "Look, why don't you just sit down."

Someone behind me called out, "Sit the fuck down, motherfucker!"

Then someone else shouted, "Answer the man's question!"

Things were obviously getting out of control, as my fellow lifers now tried to egg on a confrontation. Painfully, I knew I would have to remain standing until I got an answer, no matter what happened.

The third man, who had said nothing so far, finally broke his silence. "Look, all of this noise is going to get the guards into our business." Then he addressed me, "Now look, I ain't never seen you at a meeting before. I don't even know if you're really a lifer. Besides, we ain't got this month's statement yet."

The three then began to speak among themselves. The tallest one had to be pulled back from advancing toward me.

Before I got a chance to decide what to do, I was pulled down into my seat by the smiling man. He never gave me a chance to speak.

"You are either the bravest man I have ever met or the dumbest. It's too early to tell which." This wasn't said offensively, and the man's demeanor was so kindly that I had to appreciate his sense of humor. But I still kept one eye on the three speakers.

"Now just sit where you're at and try not to say anything," he continued. "You made your point. What you need to do now is take a look behind you and see what you got started. Those three guys up there are really not your major problem."

Cautiously I glanced back. I was surprised to see how many men were standing up and looking in our direction. There was a lot of cursing, mumbling, and even a few snarls. I turned back around.

"What are they all so mad about?"

"Mad?" The smiling man belly-laughed. "They're not mad. They're just warming up."

Almost on cue, one of the men directly behind us stood up and hollered, "You know *I'm* a lifer, motherfucker, now you tell me about that money. And don't give me no shit about you don't know. You ain't pulling that on me. This ain't my first time here."

Someone else shouted out, "Man, don't be feeding into that negative shit. Sit the fuck down!"

Yet another voice called out, "Man, fuck that! What's wrong with knowing how much money we got?"

The guy directly behind me answered, "They stealing, that's what's wrong."

"So who ain't?" shouted a faraway voice.

A dozen men were now arguing among themselves, some holding others back. It looked like a fight was about to break out at any minute. Nevertheless, my companion just continued to smile as he shook his head.

"It sure doesn't take much to get these men started," he said.

Still a little confused about what was going on, I just looked at him in silent amazement.

"Let me ask you a question," he said. "Did you happen to notice that the guard locked us all in here with no supervision? Do you know why he did that?"

I shook my head.

"Because he knows that everybody in this room has at least one confirmed homicide to his credit. And obviously being smarter than us both, he decided he didn't want to be caught in a dark room alone with a bunch of murderers who might start fighting. Now tell me, what do you suggest we do if things turn ugly?"

His words left me speechless.

"I thought so. You haven't got a plan. You're just playing out of pocket. Well then, you might as well tell me your name so, if I get my old behind in a tussle, I'll know who to thank."

It took me a moment to answer. "My name's Victor, but I really didn't mean . . ."

"It's too late to sweat it now. I just hope you can fight as good as you can talk, because you managed to embarrass some of the men in here."

"But all I did was ask a question."

"That's all it takes in this place. People don't like to answer a whole lot of questions, especially about money, especially if they're stealing. I'd be surprised if they weren't. By the way, my name is Harold, but I prefer to be called Omar. I don't like being called by my slave name." With that he extended his hand to me.

I gladly shook Omar's hand. It looked like I might be needing a friend. Besides, there was something about him that I really liked and admired. Nothing seemed to rattle him.

To our relief, things were settling down. Almost everybody was sitting down now, though with a cautious edge.

"Why does everyone seem so angry all the time?" I asked my new friend.

"Good question. It's probably because most of the men in here take everything personally. Nothing's really personal unless you want it to be. Or it could be that anger is really all the authorities leave you that's your own. They take everything else away from you at Receiving. Now, why don't we start easing toward the door so that, when the guard decides to open up, we can slip out of here without getting our feelings hurt."

With that sage advice, Omar and I got up and walked up the aisle. He was smiling and chuckling, which took some of the tension out of the air, occasionally calling out or waving to one of his friends.

Once we made it to the auditorium door, Omar turned to me and said, "Victor, you live a charmed life. You may even manage to come out of this with a little rep [reputation]. In the future, try not to upset anybody and always make sure you have a way out before you start asking questions. Frankly, you like things a little too exciting for me."

In time, Omar and I became as close as brothers. The population would come to know us collectively as the Muslim and the Jew. And it was through Omar's wisdom that I learned that nothing in prison is personal.

Chapter 7

Race Relations in Prison

Editors' Note

Race is a constant in many prisons. An inmate's race may determine where he can stand, sit, or work, or what he can say and to whom. In many prisons, race-based rules of behavior are common, and minor infractions of the rules can have serious consequences. Knowing these rules is part of becoming a convict. As one might suspect, race-based rules lie in the purview of the prison's political system and are part of the status quo. But as Hassine points out, race can be transcended by other factors.

Race relations between prisoners and guards are a more complicated issue. Other things being equal, the racial make-up of a prison's staff is determined by the racial make-up of the locale. Thus, prisons located in rural areas tend to have predominately white staffs, while urban prisons tend to have racially mixed or even predominately black staffs. This generalization usually excludes the effects of affirmative action programs, unions, and organizational philosophies, which can further complicate any sociological analysis of prisoner–guard race relations.

> ". . . A gang leader in Philadelphia has led Graterford's Muslim movement, officials said, controlling part of the prison's drug trade. A prison guard, Lieutenant Cynthia Link, said that when the lights in the prison's mosque suddenly went out one night two years ago, the 100 inmates ignored her order to leave. Finally, one of them said, 'Ms. Link, these people aren't going to move until [the gang leader] tells them to.' Link said, 'Well, go get him, tell him I need him.' He came, told the prisoners to leave, and they did. . . ."
>
> *The New York Times*, October 30, 1995
> [Complete article reprinted in Appendix A]

Every Pennsylvania prison that I have been to, regardless of the ratio between black and white inmates, was operated by an almost entirely white staff. In Graterford between 1981 and 1982, over 80 percent of the staff were white, while over 80 percent of the inmates were black. By July 1987, according to two Pennsylvania Department of Corrections surveys on a racial breakdown of inmates and a corrections-workforce comparison, the disparity remained relatively the same with 76 percent white staff and 76 percent black inmates. To its credit, however, Graterford employed the highest percentage of minority employees out of all of Pennsylvania's state prisons.

Though the prison had been desegregated since the late 1960s, the inmates of Graterford continued to impose their own form of segregation. For example, it was an unspoken rule that the dining hall be divided into a black section and a white section. The administration did its part as well, for example, by refusing to double-cell white inmates with black inmates. De facto segregation was very much alive in those days, as it is today.

At Graterford I observed that many of the new white guards had little experience interacting with people of different races. Presumably due to feelings of intimidation or discomfort with inmates of other races, they tended to be much stricter with those of their own race.

During my initial classification period at Graterford, I was required to identify myself as either black or white. There were no other options. Hispanics and Native Americans were classified as black or white, depending on their choice.It wasn't until the mid-1980s that the racial classification process at Graterford allowed inmates to designate themselves as anything other than black or white.

Among the African-American population at Graterford was a large and well-established Black Muslim community, the vast majority of which came from Philadelphia. On the other hand, most of the white prison staff were Christians, many of whom were raised in the rural communities around the prison. This extreme imbalance between the racial, regional, and religious composition of staff and inmates vividly reflected the general dysfunction of the prison that prevailed throughout my years there.

Though non-white inmates were usually embraced by the prison population, they were often viewed with suspicion by the white staff, who seemed to believe that only white inmates could be reformed into law-abiding citizens. This racial bias at Graterford did not result in favoritism by staff but rather provoked a divisive and relentless competition between the inmates themselves for the staff's favor. Everyone in the prison system was forced to play the bias game, because the only group identity available to inmates was based on skin color.

As a rule, a prison administration is reluctant to promote any group activity or identity that might evolve into cliques or gangs. Graterford's sole purpose was custody, so its entire security force was geared toward discouraging and punishing any group affiliations. All inmates were issued identical uniforms, and there were strictly enforced rules against any congregation of more than five inmates. While some social and religious organizations were permitted to operate, the administration made the rules of participation so cumbersome that these groups constituted organizations in names only. Though the prison could not punish an inmate for belonging to a legitimate group, it could try to weaken his desire to belong. One of the ways in which this was accomplished was to influence every inmate, including myself, in the direction of racial polarization.

Black and White Prison Gangs

Generally, black gangs in Graterford were extensions of Philadelphia's neighborhood street gangs. They bore names based on their urban location; for example, the 21st and Norris Gang, the 60th and Market Gang, the 10th Street Gang, etc. Many of their members had belonged to the original street gang before they were incarcerated. Once sent to Graterford, they joined their prison counterpart to carry on the gang's traditions. As more and more street-gang members arrived, their growing strength in numbers enabled them to conduct a wider array of prison-gang activities.

The moment any African-American Philadelphian entered the prison, scouts immediately approached him to determine which part of the city he came from and whether he had been a member of a street gang. This sorting of incoming blacks based on geography dictated the character of black prison gangs, giving rise to the often used term "homey" for those who hailed from the same neighborhood or hometown. Homeys were the most common recruits for black-gang membership.

Black gangs competed vigorously with each other for turf and the control of contraband sales. While this competition often resulted in violent battles, gangs on many occasions merged their enterprises and worked together. For example, rival gangs had been known to fight each other over the business of selling drugs, yet they frequently cooperated in bringing the drugs into the prison.

Those black gangs formed by inmates from areas other than Philadelphia differed considerably from the black Philly gangs in that, for the most part, they had no counterparts on the streets. Such non-Philly gangs usually originated in the prison and their members were often strangers who happened to be from the same county or city. The competition between regional gangs and Philly gangs tended to be very hostile and violent. There was seldom any trust or cooperation between them. Numerically, Philly gangs greatly outnumbered other gangs, which allowed them to dominate the population and completely exclude outsiders from joint ventures.

Regardless of their numerical superiority, it is highly probable that Philly gangs still would have had more control, because their carry-over from street gangs gave them the distinct advantage of functioning under well-established rules, organizational structures, leadership systems, and ideologies. In contrast, regional or prison-based gangs tended to be weakened internally by frequent power struggles, uncertain leadership, and untested organizational processes.

Because Graterford's black gangs were determined almost exclusively by geography, gang membership was widely diverse. In any one gang you could expect to find drug addicts, thieves, murderers, and hustlers of every stripe, including Muslims, Christians, and atheists. This amalgam of homeys provided black-gang members with such strength and vitality that the administration was hard pressed to break them apart.

Black gangs at Graterford primarily operated as money-making enterprises. While geography helped to bring prison gang members together, it was money and drugs that kept them together. The goal of every gang was to earn money, which meant selling anything that anyone was willing to buy. As in a corporation, gang profits were then reinvested to buy more contraband for further distribution. Gang members gauged their individual value by the amount of money they were able to make. What they did with their earnings was of no consequence, since the hustle itself seemed to be all that mattered. Money earned was merely an indicator of how good a hustler an inmate could be.

White gangs at Graterford were a completely different story. These gangs almost always originated in prison and, like the non-Philly gangs, were not as well-structured or established. They too were comprised of members who were often strangers to each other, most of them brought together by the simple chance of their skin color.

Statistically, white gangs in Graterford were strictly a minority, usually formed for their own protection from other gangs. While they might be involved in some hustling, they were limited by their inability to protect their turf or business interests against the larger black gangs. They were more likely to be the buyers of drugs and contraband than the sellers.

Furthermore, most white gang members were not brought together by geography but rather out of a need to protect their mutual interests. White drug addicts tended to join together in order to pool their funds to buy drugs at a volume discount. Some white gangs were formed because of ethnic bonds, such as Catholics, Italians, and Protestants, or because of special interests, such as gamblers and body builders.

White gangs at Graterford were more likely to be small, improvised groups rather than organized teams with specific agendas, and were generally much less diverse than their black counterparts. Whereas black gangs required large memberships to generate income and protect their turf, white gangs preferred to have as few members as possible in an effort to stretch their resources. Any white gang that grew too large would promptly be challenged by the dominant black gangs.

The exceptions in Graterford were the outlaw motorcycle gangs that successfully managed to entrench themselves within the prison system. Like the Hell's Angels who had already established themselves on the street, they were far more business-oriented and could compete directly with black gangs in the sale of contraband, drugs in particular. Despite their relatively small numbers in the prison, their connections to the much larger street gangs made them resourceful money-makers and a power to be reckoned with.

The Muslim and the Jew

Not long after my first Lifers meeting, Omar became my closest friend and my window into the workings of prison life. He knew many of the inmates at Graterford and understood better than I the language, games, players, and dangers of the prison system. Most importantly, he was willing to share his wisdom with me. His profound insight into the system helped me to grope my way through a foreign country of which I had had no inkling before I arrived at Graterford. Thus, Omar became my Old Head and I became his eager disciple.

A few months after I had lost my job in the Major's office, Omar was hired to take my place. Since he now lived on the same block as I did, I often visited him in his cell. We ate meals together, walked the yard together, and exchanged a lot of jailhouse philosophy to kill time. We became inseparable and were one of the more unusual sights in Graterford: the veteran black Muslim from Philadelphia and the young Jewish rookie from New Jersey. We were constantly arguing about one issue or another.

I would often find my Old Head sitting on the cold, hard concrete floor of his cell, deeply absorbed in writing a letter to his family but never turning his back to the doorway, always keeping one cautious eye on the inmate traffic a few feet away. His cell was drab and spartan, containing little more than state-issued clothing, bedding, and some old newspapers. I once asked Omar why he chose to have so few possessions.

"I don't like people taking things away from me," he replied. "If I don't have anything in here that's mine, then the authorities can't take away any more than they already have. Besides, I don't think it's healthy for a man to get too comfortable in the slammer."

On one occasion I had just returned from a prison basketball game that had ended in a vicious melee between a black and a white gang. Often one prison gang would field a team to play against a team backed by another gang, and the rivalry on the court usually led to violence. Watching who won the game was only half as exciting as watching who won the fight *after* the game.

But today I was particularly disturbed by the rampant hatred and racism between black and white inmates, so I posed a naive question to Omar: "Why do they hate and hurt each other so much? Why don't they just get together and channel their hatred toward the guards?"

Omar's ubiquitous grin vanished. After a long stare that was pregnant with pause, he finally said: "It's all a game."

"What, that's it?" I protested. "All the beatings, stabbings, and killings are just a game? It's no game. Men dying is no game."

Omar regarded me with some amazement. I must have been a bit more excited than I had intended. With a gentle but serious tone he cautioned, "Are you going to argue with me or are you going to listen?"

I sat quietly, waiting for him to share his view of the restless shadow we lived in. Just outside his cell, silent, unfriendly faces glided past, glancing inside, never smiling. It was this kind of backdrop that kept a man alert in his cell at all times. Occasionally a prison guard would look in on us and then move on. Though I was not allowed to enter another man's cell, the rule was never enforced.

"Most of the hate and anger in here is all a game," Omar emphasized again. "It's a hustle, just another way for people to make money. Anger and hatred are a prison's cash crop.

"When whites hate blacks, they're stealing the sympathy and favor of a mostly white Christian administration. When blacks hate whites, they're strong-arming appeasements and concessions. The administration, they get the most out of it all. Violence and hatred in prison means more money, more guards, more overtime, and more prisons. What incentive is there to keep prisons safe and humane? All staff has to do is sit back and let the men here tear each other apart. Then they can cry to the legislatures and tell them how much more money they need to control their prison. Just like with the prison swag men, dope boys, and laundry men, there's something being sold and money being made. Only it's a lot more money than most of the guys in here can ever imagine. It's a lot easier for everyone to profit from hatred than it is to help the poor and ignorant do something positive with their lives."

I couldn't believe what I was hearing. "Come on, Omar, you can't believe that stuff. You're sounding real paranoid, like there's a conspiracy everywhere." His views were similar to those of Double D, who believed the administration was actually encouraging gang activity. But I wasn't ready to believe either one of them. The prison system was too chaotic to be that deliberate.

Omar replied, "Well, then you tell me why, with all the guards, guns, locks, gates, walls, and money, they still can't stop what's going on in here?"

I had no answer to that. "Okay, if this is all a game and everybody knows it, then why do the men in here play it? Why do they play when it can get them hurt and even killed?"

Omar smiled assuredly. "It's like a Dodge City crap game in here, Victor. Everyone who plays it knows it's crooked, but they play it anyway—because it's the only game in town."

Chapter 8

Saying Goodbye

It was a hot summer day one particular weekend. Most of the inmates were wearing non-prison sweat suits, sweat shirts, or ragtag gym clothes homemade from scraps of stolen cloth. Many of them chose to spend all their recreation time on the block, most of them serious gamblers or avoiding the sun or avoiding a fight.

The gamblers were the easiest to spot because they always played cards on the most private picnic tables in the deepest interior. To a man, they slumped low in their seats, ready at a moment's notice to reach for their weapons. These weapons were usually hidden somewhere below the table, waiting for someone to be caught cheating or prematurely grabbing another man's money. Most other block loungers just milled around, talking, smoking, or drinking coffee as if they were somewhere other than in a maximum security prison.

I had just returned to my cell to change into state whites for my infirmary job. To me, the only difference between hard labor and imposed idleness is the change in a man's appearance. In the end, both will break a man's spirit as surely as his sentence will make him older.

As I left my cell, I heard a distant commotion from the upper range. Hearing it too, the table gamblers slumped a little deeper in their seats, easing closer to their weapons, their eyes never leaving their cards.

Soon I could make out an inmate called Hammerhead Fred, running toward me down the narrow walkway of the tier above, with guards in hot pursuit. He was carrying a five-gallon plastic bag, the kind used to dispense milk from a cafeteria cooler with a rubber nipple on one end. But this one was filled with homemade jailhouse hootch.

As he ran the length of a football field, Hammerhead lifted the bag over his head and forced the booze to flow into his open mouth. Much of it poured onto his face and chest, glazing his protruding forehead and staining his dirty clothes. The heavy bootlegged load was slowing him down, and the pursuing guards were gaining on him.

The whole cellblock was in an uproar, every man cheering him on. "Go Hammerhead! Fuck those hacks! Drink that wine! Don't give it up! Hammerhead! Hammerhead! Hammerhead!"

Just as the lead guard caught up to Hammerhead, an inmate suddenly stepped out of his cell and "accidentally" collided with the guard. The two fell down, and the other guards toppled over them in Keystone Kops fashion.

This gave Hammerhead enough time to take an extra long swallow of hootch. Then he jumped off the second-story walkway and landed upright on a tabletop below. Amazingly, he managed to hold onto his five-gallon bag. His legs spread boldly across the table, Hammerhead guzzled more wine until he had had his fill. Then he hurled the container at the frenzied crowd around him, beat his chest, and gave a savage victory cry.

The crowd screamed, hollered, and beat their chests as they drank from the contraband container, passing it from man to man in a victory-sharing ritual. Finally, the guards got themselves together enough to force Hammerhead down from the table. The inmates booed and hissed as they escorted Hammerhead away, no doubt to a waiting cell in the Hole.

But Hammerhead couldn't have cared less, because he was too drunk to feel any pain and more importantly because today was his last day in captivity. He had served all ten years of his sentence, and he owed no parole time or probation. He was out tomorrow, free and clear.

This was how Hammerhead wanted to be remembered and how he would always be remembered. This is also how I have always remembered Graterford and its Kingdom of Inmates, since the day I myself said goodbye and good riddance to its wretched concrete walls.

PART II

Interviews

Editors' Note

In this second section, Victor Hassine presents a series of interviews with fellow inmates, each with a specific theme. These personal views serve to broaden the author's perspective on prison life. Readers should be aware that in some cases the interviews have been edited to disguise and to protect the true identities of the interviewees, but otherwise the interviews are largely verbatim.

Chapter 9

David: A Sexual Victim

Editors' Note

The following interview with David is a troubling piece. The interview was intended not to pass judgment but to portray accurately a man's transformation from youthful innocence to a life of victimization. The catalyst here is what Hassine has called "senseless violence," of which David is a sad product.

I first met David, my current next-door cell neighbor, in Graterford. He was starting a two-to-five-year sentence, and I was two years into my life sentence. David was 19 then and "cute as a bug in a rug"—a curse for any young man in prison.

At the time, I was working as a clerk in the Chapel, which was how I met David. It was there that he was assaulted and raped repeatedly by at least three men. I was present to see the aftermath of young David's introduction into Graterford's criminal justice system, one of many lessons on the facts of life in prison society.

It is now about ten years later. This is David's second time back in prison, my fourth transfer to a different institution. We both have landed in SCI-Rockview, which is a medium/minimum security prison in the mountainous central region of Pennsylvania. Rockview is considered to be one of the less restrictive "soft stops" in the Pennsylvania state prison system.

It was here not too long ago that another attractive young man like David was gang-raped by four of his weight-lifting buddies.

The head "booty bandit" [jailhouse rapist] was named Pac Man, also a cute-looking youth when he first rolled into Graterford to do his time. Ironically, the same "beef rustlers" who raped David in the Chapel had also "long-dicked" Pac Man a year or two earlier. This is but one of many examples of prison's vicious cycle of victims-turned-attackers.

David was gang-raped not once but twice. Now in his late twenties, he has served close to half his life in institutions and has made most of the important decisions of his life based on the experience interacting with inmates.

David's story, a grim portrait of today's incarcerated youth, presents a too-common slice of prison life that is sadder than that of many of the broken men who are my neighbors, and sadder still than the prison pallor that greets me in the mirror every morning. The following is excerpted from a 1991 interview.

"[In the county jail I had] sexual pressure, fighting over my manhood. I was playing chess for money and lost several times, and it became like a 20- or 30-dollar debt. I couldn't immediately cover it. I was given a choice, either borrow it or have sex with him. We got into a fight. [After that] he left me alone. . . .

"There were a couple of guys who tried to take me under their wings, but I didn't really trust them. I had heard stories about this. The ones who wanted to take me under their wing I didn't even know until I went to jail. It was strictly a con; [these guys] were like predators. . . .

"When I got to Graterford, I took protective custody lock-up 24 hours a day. A guard came down one day who had a pass for me to go get legal mail. He unlocked my door and left. I got up out of bed in my underwear and was rushed by approximately six or more inmates. I was raped numerous times. They rushed me, then threw me to the floor and hit me a few times. Before I had a chance to react, a knife was placed at my neck. I was already on my side or stomach. I don't remember what was said. I somewhat knew what they wanted and it wasn't my commissary. All they did was fuck me with no emotion. I was hoping while this was happening that they would ask me to have oral sex and I would then bite them. Had it been under other circumstances, I would have fought back. At that time I was in good shape. I would guess logically that it was a 'set up.' They left as soon as it was over. I was angry, bleeding, and in quite a bit of pain. Because I was in protective custody and it happened there, the point in telling or reporting it was pointless and also very dangerous. . . .

"I lost all hope for about six months. I was totally stripped of emotion. I just didn't give a fuck anymore. When I was much younger, I was a vengeful person. But I didn't want to get even because where there is an action, there is always a reaction. . . .

"I don't think it was fair that I was raped, because I did nothing to deserve the vicious assault that has haunted my mind for almost ten years. They had no right to victimize me, and now I have become a product of that assault. It has caused me to become attracted to other young men sexually, so as to continue the nightmare by further subjecting myself to punishment for my past crimes, and to also inflict my nightmare on others so they too can carry the terrible burden I've carried. . . .

"The administration could have done more to protect me, or others that are in protective custody, by totally segregating them, which ultimately wouldn't be fair, because you would be deprived of all activities enjoyed by the regular inmates. But, on the other hand, isn't this the same reason most of us are here, for depriving those of society of their normal routines and enjoyments of life? Basically these types of occurrences can be avoided by tighter security for these young individuals, because most of the booty bandits are already known by the administration. Again, these occurrences are so commonplace that the administration often looks the other way, unless the person who is victimized is willing to put his life on the line and prosecute the perpetrators. The reason I say the perpetrators, instead of the guilty ones or rapers, is because most of these individuals are the victims of violence themselves. . . .

"After the first time I was raped while in protective custody, I convinced the officials to let me out in population without telling them that I was assaulted. They let me out into population and I ran into a friend who I met on the street. I hung around with him for a while, figuring he could teach me the ropes of survival in the "Big House." He introduced me to a fellow who was too nice, who one day invited me to the Chapel to get high. I met him, and he had a few friends with him. We smoked a couple of joints, and the next thing I knew I was getting physically beaten and again was viciously raped by at least three guys. . . .

"After I was raped, the only medical attention that I received was a physical examination of my rectum to confirm that I had been assaulted. I was placed back in protective custody by myself without anyone to talk to, alone and deserted like a dirty rag. I received no therapy from either a psychologist or a psychiatrist. I was left to deal with it on my own. I didn't cry out then because no one seemed to care, and so I stripped myself of all and any emotions. If there were people who cared, they really didn't come forward, which is natural, because it is a very difficult thing to respond to. I can sympathize with women victims. It is a devastating experience to not only cope with, but even more to live with. . . .

"Once I was released from prison, I was very demanding of people because I felt they owed me something. And more than often, if my wishes were not complied with, I took what I desired from them. Don't get me wrong, I never raped anyone, but I did lash out on all the supposed predators and even those, both family and friends, who I felt deserved to be tormented. I didn't discriminate. I did it to anyone I felt had it coming to them. Anyway, that was how sick I was then, or rather that was how obsessed I was, until recently. Now, mostly I feel guilty about what I've done in an act of retaliation. But I also realize I was really crying for help in the only way I could, by acting out.

"I am a very confused person now, sexually that is, because I am insecure about what is natural combined with what I've been through and seen with my own eyes through the many years that I've been in institutions, 13 years altogether. I am attracted to younger guys because of their innocent look and naive personalities, more so because it's that very innocence that I was robbed of. Sometimes I feel really guilty after I have sex with a guy, because I know or feel that I have violated their minds subconsciously, and eventually they'll have to face the music about who they are or cop out and remain a victim. But I am realizing that all that is happening is that I am doing it because that's the only way I can get any kind of love, affection, and attention that I so desperately need.

"[As for the system], I still don't trust them because they are the true predators and rapers of the people."

David is getting out soon. I wonder whether he will find that desperately needed love, affection, and attention in the outside world. And if he doesn't, I wonder what he will do.

Chapter 10

Chaser: A Medication Addict

Editors' Note

Prescription medications are ubiquitous in many prisons, and chlor-promazine tranquilizers are common in virtually all these institutions. Other medications, such as amphetamines, barbiturates, and diazopene tranquilizers, are routinely dispensed. Although these medications are given to inmates under the supervision of a physician, the actual distribution is often handled by guards and fellow prisoners. Since these prescription medications are readily available, their role in the underground economy is small. Any prisoner with a prescription can hoard pills, of course, and sell or give them to others.

The author's opinion of prescription medications and their use in American prisons is apparent in his interview with Chaser. Whether one agrees with him or not, medications have become part of the status quo in most prisons. Given the increasing use of penal institutions for housing the mentally ill, it is unlikely that the prevalence of prescription medications will abate in the near future.

I met Chaser in 1984, my fourth year at Graterford, when he first arrived to serve time on a robbery conviction. I can still remember the frightened look on his face that first day. As I was adapting to the rapidly changing rules and conditions of a prison in total meltdown, Chaser became the beneficiary of my hard-learned lessons on inmate survival. We managed to forge a mutual friendship.

Many outsiders who have met Chaser would comment, "He doesn't look like he belongs in here." I've heard this often when people encounter an inmate who doesn't have some grotesque feature that neatly fits their preconceived notion of the "criminal look." Experience has taught me that the less an inmate appears like a criminal, the more likely he is to be particularly vicious and unrepentant. Criminals who look like criminals keep people on guard; the honest-looking ones put them at ease, which allows them the greater advantage of misjudgment. But in Chaser's case they were right. He didn't belong in prison, let alone deserve to become a victim of the system.

I did my best to look after my friend until, about nine months later, he was transferred to the Rockview facility. This was a relief for me, since protecting a naive and scared young man from the predators at Graterford was no easy task.

Once he was transferred, I quickly forgot about Chaser. Frankly, it is nearly impossible for me to remember all the people that have come in and out of my life, especially nowadays with the influx of so many frightened young kids. Almost all my relations with fellow inmates today are superficial, as prison life becomes more and more a case of every man for himself.

What Chaser and I didn't know at the time was that prison administrators were feverishly trying to figure out how to stop the imminent collapse of Graterford and other overcrowded prisons. With thousands of new, young Chasers coming in, it was becoming more impossible to feed, house, and clothe them all, let alone rehabilitate them. More importantly to officials, an increasing number of guards and staff were becoming victims of inmate attacks. As employee safety was their first priority, the administrators realized that something had to be done to shore up the cracks in Graterford's foundation—and it had to be quick, cheap, and effective. But Chaser and I never concerned ourselves with the administration's problems. After all, we had swag men to deal with and predators to avoid.

In 1990, as I made my way to chow at Rockview, I ran into Chaser again. He was walking out of the dining hall's special section reserved for the "nuts," whom the administration refer to euphemistically as "special-needs inmates." Chaser walked sluggishly with a disheveled, glassy-eyed appearance. In short, he *looked* like one of the nuts.

"Chaser, is that you?" I asked.

"Hey, Vic," he replied, "I've got to talk to you. It's real important. Meet me in the yard."

That evening in the yard, my old friend explained to me how he had returned to the streets two years earlier, only to lose his wife and son, develop a voracious drug habit, and end up committing burglaries to support his habit.

I was unmoved by Chaser's story, since almost every returning con I've ever met recounts a similar tale of woe. All I wanted to know was why he was on the nut block and why he was taking "brake fluid" [prescribed psychotropic medication]. It was obvious because of his very slow, disjointed movement and his shakes. Another alarming clue was the noticeable scars on his wrists from razor cuts.

Chaser described how his return to prison had exposed him to the "medicate-and-forget-them" system of modern prison management. This new system of mind-altering and mood-altering psychotropic drugs was rapidly becoming the prison administration's "quick, cheap, and effective" solution to warehousing masses of inmates into smaller spaces, while using fewer and fewer support services.

The reasoning seemed to be that every dose of medication taken by an inmate equaled one less fraction of a guard needed to watch that inmate, and one less inmate who may pose a threat to anyone other than himself. Hence, overcrowding had brought about a merging of the psychiatric and corrections communities. The resulting effect on inmates can be best described by Chaser during this 1994 interview.

"The first time [I came to prison] I was terrified because I didn't know what to expect and I knew no one. I was awkward and didn't know my way around. I had not acquired a prison or inmate mentality. The second time I was much more at ease because I knew a lot of people still in prison and I knew what to expect. I had also learned quite fast how to become as comfortable as possible. I had to take a lot of psychotropic drugs to achieve this comfortable state of mind. . . .

"In November of 1989, after telling the shrink in the county prison that I wished I was dead, I was unknowingly given Sinequan which knocked me out for three days. But since I was in a special quiet section of the jail, I continued the medication, because to me it was better than being in population. . . .

"I think the biggest difference between street drugs and psychotropic drugs is that street drugs give me some kind of feeling of well-being, high, confidence, euphoria, and contentment. But psychotropic drugs cause all feeling to cease. It stops self-awareness and sucks the soul out of a man. It slows or stops a man from striving to better himself and he stops caring about everything. It also creates total laziness. That laziness becomes his entire attitude and also is 100-percent habit-forming. . . .

"After almost three months at the county prison in Philly, I was sent to Graterford to start my four-to-ten-year sentence. I had abruptly stopped taking the Sinequan and felt totally disoriented. I lasted three weeks in population. Looking for drugs, I ended up taking another inmate's Thorazine at times. I was out of control and all I could think of or look forward to was getting stoned.

"One day I got very drunk and went into a blackout and refused to lock up. Four guards carried me to a room and I was put into restraints. I was given nine months in the Hole. I did five at Graterford and was sent to Rockview to complete it. . . .

"[Getting medication in Rockview] was quite easy. I said I wished I was dead, which was the same thing I said in the county. Every week the shrink would ask, 'How do you feel now?' All I had to do was say, 'Bad,' and ask for more or different meds. I always got what I asked for, as long as I told them I thought of killing myself. . . . I took Sinequan, Melloril, Elavil, Klonopin, first separately, while always asking for Valium. Then in desperation, I mixed the medications and the dosages. The ultimate effect was total numbness. My body was numb. My feelings were numb, and then my mind was numb. I did not care what happened to me and just stopped thinking about anything. . . .

"While taking the meds, I was put on a special block and given a single cell. I got only a reprimand at misconduct hearings and did not have to go to work. I felt I was being placated and given special attention and I liked that. But when I stopped taking the meds, I was shook down [cell-searched] a lot and went to the Hole if I was ever given a misconduct. Once in the Hole, I would say I wish I was dead, and again they'd give me medication. . . .

"I admitted to staff many times that I had a severe drug addiction and that I had an abusive personality. I tried numerous times to get in the drug-therapy groups and on the D and A [Drug and Alcohol] Blocks. I was refused and ignored every time. . . .

"I lost all sense of dignity and self-worth. I had no pride. I lost all interest in the outside world and eventually did not care if I ever returned to it. All I knew or cared about was what times I went to get my fix. . . . [I] hurried to be first in line. I constantly had the shakes and inner tremors. My speech was slurred and slowed, and so was my thinking. I could not think ahead. I was like a small child only looking for instant gratification. My entire metabolism changed, and I gained a lot of weight fast. It damaged my memory, even to this day. . . .

"Since I was under constant supervision and being evaluated once or twice a month, pre-release and parole became much harder to obtain. So for the luxury of being comfortable and in a fantasy world, I had to abandon the idea of early release or furloughs. Since my number-one priority was no longer a goal, it became easy for me to forget or stop striving for what was once important to me. The side effects of the medication, such as tremors and shakes, made it impossible for me to get and keep a job. Education, reading, learning, and working to strengthen my mind became things of the past. Giving up became repetitious and habit-forming (not unlike street drugs) and eventually I lost and gave up my self-respect, dignity, and morals until my only interest in life was getting in line three times a day to receive my medication.

"I had given up on all these things, and I woke up one day and realized I was a very sad man. But I was willing to give up on life, because the medications I was taking made me think I was comfortable. . . . I had given up on Chaser. . . .

"I was seeing a shrink two times a week because I was depressed. I was not diagnosed as having any kind of mental illness or chemical imbalance, but despite that I was taking large dosages of Thorazine, Sinequan, Lithium, Elavil, and Melloril. I took them at 7 a.m., 11 a.m., 4 p.m., 8 p.m. . . .

"One night just before lockup, I got another misconduct. I didn't care if I went to the Hole or got cell restriction. What concerned me was that the administration might possibly take away my medication. So after weighing my options, it seemed only logical to kill myself, or at the least, give that appearance. I opened my window, pressed my wrists against the frozen bars, then took an old razor and opened my wrists. I figured that, if I died, that would be fine. But, if I lived, I would definitely get more medication, and that thought satisfied me. I lived this madness and insanity for well over a year, until I ran into you. You offered me your time and energy to explain to me what I was doing to myself and what I was becoming. Within six months, I was totally off the special-needs block and off 99 percent of the medication and my will to live and succeed returned . . . with a vengeance. I never needed the medications for my depressed condition. I just needed someone to say they cared. I needed a friend. I got both from you. I owe you my life, not the prison, and not the medication. . . .

"I have been medication-free for two years now and, although I'm usually uncomfortable with prison conditions, I can look in the mirror and see Chaser looking back with a smile. So to me, giving up the medication was a small price to pay to be myself again.

"[Psychotropic medication] is one of the easiest things to get in prison. It is easier to go to the shrink and ask for 500 mg of Thorazine than it is to get on the phone or get a pass to the Chapel. If a guy goes to the doc saying he feels depressed, violent, or suicidal, the doc will give him one of numerous medications. He is usually given a choice. All the medications are geared to slow a man down or fog his thinking so bad he can't think of why he's depressed, violent, or suicidal. This will continue for years, as long as he says he needs the medications to a staff person once a month. . . .

"I'd say 40 percent of the population here is taking some form of psychotropic medication. They are treated less harshly than those unmedicated. They are seen and talked to by staff much more often than those not on medications. They are given special consideration at misconduct hearings. They are permitted to come in from night yard earlier than the other inmates and, in a lot of cases, are given a single cell. When it comes to working, someone on psychotropic medication can usually pick whatever job he says he can handle. On the other hand, most of us were not required to work at all. . . .

"I believe that, when a guard or any staff member puts on a uniform, they know it stands for authority. So they demand respect and control. When someone rebels or stands up to them, they feel their authority and control is threatened and they take steps to eliminate the rebellion. They put on the appearance of power, so they act cold, mean, negative, and harsh to display this power.

"Now when a guy is on medication, the threat is almost nonexistent. They [the staff] feel safe and secure with the men that are medicated. So the use of force and display of power is not necessary, and they act more leniently to the medicated inmate. They treat these men like children. To staff, a medicated inmate is a controlled inmate. . . .

"[If all inmates were required to take psychotropic drugs], I would be shocked and scared. It would be like they were turning the prison into a brainwashing institution. I would think they had lost all control and were attempting to gain it back by stopping our wills and brains from functioning properly. I believe they are headed in that direction because of how easy the medications are to get and how many people are taking them. . . .

"I think that, as the prison populations continue to grow and grow, and a younger and more violent crowd comes in, it will become harder and harder for the administration to control all the blocks. I think they are now learning that the best way to control inmates or pacify them is to totally medicate them. It may even become a reward system."

Psychotropic drugs are nothing new to the psychiatric community, which has been using them on the mentally ill for years. However, its use in corrections as a population-management tool and behavior modifier is relatively new. The effects of prolonged use of such medication on an ever growing number of inmates are unknown.

Just from the increasing size of medication lines and the growing number of inmates doing the brake-fluid shuffle, I have observed that psychotropic medications (also known as "chemical shackles") are defining the behavior of an increasing percentage of inmates in the general population.

As politicians and bureaucrats continue to debate the loftier issues facing the criminal justice system, the mother of invention has required front-line prison administrators to quickly implement any practice that might help them to keep their prisons intact and functioning. The practice of medicating inmates is becoming popular because it has proven to be a relatively inexpensive and efficient prison-control tool. The two governing estates of custody and treatment are being pushed aside by the rising third estate of psychiatric medication.

A bureaucratic system that subdues whole populations with drugs must certainly give us pause. The wisdom of turning means into ultimate ends in this way needs to be questioned. Today in prison, I find myself longing for any glimpse of an attempt to rehabilitate, not because I believe that treatment works, but because I worry about a society that no longer cares enough to try to help.

In my opinion, today's prison managers are only interested in their ability to confine an ever-increasing number of people for an ever-longer period of time. Since there is only so much that can be done in terms of cell and prison design, the search for solutions has focused not on changing the nature of prisons but on changing the nature of prisoners.

As of this interview, Chaser has been off medication for about two years. He has successfully gone through drug-rehabilitation therapy and is soon due for release. Once released, he will join a growing number of mind-altered men who are leaving prison and entering the mainstream of society. Only time will tell whether chemically treated inmates do in fact make law-abiding citizens. But, if you ask me, we should go back to trying to build a better mouse trap and, for God's sake, leave the mice alone.

Chapter 11

Toney: An AIDS Tragedy

Editors' Note

Although the proportion of gay inmates is unknown, it is most likely greater than the proportion of gay men in free society. This disparity is observed despite a pattern of benign discrimination against gays in many prisons. For example, openly gay prisoners are often denied access to programming and employment opportunities "for their own protection." This pattern has expanded steadily since the onset of the AIDS epidemic. In this context, the following interview with Toney provides rare insights into the mind of an openly gay inmate. Readers with personal experience with AIDS prevention may recognize the air of despair in Toney's words, while others may by shocked by his explicit frankness.

Toney is a young homosexual inmate dying of AIDS in a Pennsylvania prison. In his own words, he takes us through the gauntlet of prison life which has beaten down his spirit with all its ordeals of love and hate, crime and punishment, and compassion and indifference.

Unlike the multitude of other incurable diseases afflicting mankind, AIDS not only threatens our emotional and physical well-being but tears at the very fabric of our society. It is for this reason that AIDS can devastate the uninfected living as mercilessly as it already has its living dead. Equally ominous is how AIDS has served as a catalyst to the social changes brought about by the ills of promiscuity, drug addiction, crime, violence, and incarceration.

In this 1992 interview, Toney relates how the lack of education about AIDS affects homosexual activity in prison, and how AIDS is used among the inmate population as a tool for self-destructive love or as a weapon of hatred that can be deadlier than a concealed knife.

"My being gay in prison [has put] a lot of pressure on me from men constantly wanting to have sex with me because of the way I look, which is on the attractive side. They constantly beg me for either a blow job or anal sex and are most of the time willing to pay for it. A gay person can be treated like royalty in prison. Homosexuals have the choice of making it easy or tough. . . .

"It is very easy to have sex in prison, at least for me it was and is. The only difference that varies from prison to prison is where you may have to do it and how careful you have to be about being caught; for example, at Graterford you could lay up all day with another man and have sex without being bothered by the C.O.'s [correction officers]. Whereas, [at Rockview] you're lucky to get a good nonstop fifteen minutes of sex. Yet it still happens. Some days in prison I have 20 men a day. . . .

"I can surmise when I may have contracted [AIDS], but I cannot say for sure. I've been an active IV drug user for 21 years, a homosexual all my life, and had a blood transfusion in 1985 before there was the start of screening blood. So you see, I cannot pinpoint it and I've had thousands of sexual partners and most of them were for one-time shots or one night only, and I used to prostitute. I do know when I first got sick in the fall of 1986. I had a tremendous loss of weight and night sweats. I had all the symptoms and that was while I was in the Philadelphia Detention Center. . . .

"I had the test taken in 1987. I was a little stunned, but I was expecting my blood test to come back positive. Why? Because of the impact of the symptoms I had in 1986 at the Detention Center. . . . The reason I say I was only stunned was that, at the time I was told, I didn't realize the seriousness of what I had. . . . A normal person's T-cell count is 2,000 or more. Mine is down to 88, and I am considered to have full-blown AIDS. . . .

"The prison administration didn't give me any support when I was first told. No physical or psychological help. I was only told to stop having sex and that, if I was caught having sex, they would put me in the Hole. They did nothing to help me in any way for the remainder of the 18 months I had left to do. I didn't get any help until I went home and went to a specialist who prescribed AZT and Bactium to try and prolong my life. That's when I realized the seriousness of my illness and that it was a matter of life or death. . . .

"I sincerely believe [the prison administration] should have more accurately informed me—by the proper medical staff—of what I had and what could happen or couldn't happen. There should have been more facts given to me than the words 'don't have sex.' With this type of illness, a person, or I should say myself, should have been more educated on what was necessary to try to maintain life for as long as I could and the prevention of getting sicker. And as a result of just being told not to have sex—without strict reasons—I continued to have sex and more than likely infected others who infected others. At the time I was not aware that AIDS could so easily be passed from one person to another. I believed that you could not get it from oral sex or that sex with the same partner only a few times was safe. I was wrong because of the lack of education, or should I say no education, from the prison administration. If they can tell you you're slowly dying, they should also give you the facts as to what can harm others as well as harm yourself. . . . I remained sexually active [for two years] until I was educated by doctors on the street and read and educated myself about AIDS. . . .

"I now realize the dangers that are involved in having unprotected sex. So, therefore, I have made it a practice to be honest and direct with anyone who asks me about my condition, whether it be a sexual partner or someone asking out of curiosity. I explain as well as inform others of the risk involved in dealing with someone like me, with the illness that I have. Even as I warn them, my partners usually don't care whether they get it or not. All they're concerned about is loving me or making love to me. I have allowed myself to be in relationships where no protection was used, and it is not because I did not tell them. It is because they wanted to be a part of me and make lifelong commitments to me. Or they wanted a lifelong commitment from me. So once they started having unprotected sex with me, it was my spouse's way of saying, 'You belong to me forever.'

"This happened with my last spouse whom I love very much, and we didn't use anything. So he now has [AIDS] and he knew all the risks. Yet he wanted it that way, so I allowed it to happen. He has a life sentence and he wanted to die and lay side by side with me in a coffin when I die. He did it out of love, and I thought I let it happen out of love. I realize that what we did was the insanity of being human beings. We were both wrong, or more so me, for allowing it to happen. But there's a saying, 'love can sometimes be blinding,' and in this case it was true. Because I loved him, and yet I hurt him. I learned not to let my emotions overcome my reality. . . .

"I know some associates of mine who are out to get revenge on people and are passing [AIDS] on. A homosexual I know says he is going to kill as many people as possible. I'll never understand it, but that is the way human nature is and the way some of us accept or cannot accept life's situations. It happened and there is very little chance of a person knowing whom to hurt anyway. So they want everyone to hurt as they hurt. I myself may have gotten AIDS because of someone not caring and out to kill everyone else. I'll never know. . . .

"I am doing this [interview] of my own free will, because I care for human life. Also so I may make people more aware [that] . . . a person [who] is HIV positive can feel, cope, and deal with it. Also to enlighten the minds of others with or without AIDS. And to let people know that prison is not a way of life and AIDS is not either and is no joke. . . .

"[If I were standing in front of the Governor of Pennsylvania], I would first tell him that it should be mandatory to ask inmates if they want to be tested for the HIV virus. Not mandatory testing, but mandatory to ask inmates if they want to be tested for the HIV virus. That way it can stop the spreading of a lot of illness and death in prison, because a lot of inmates have it and don't know it because they're not tested. Even though the administration doesn't condone homosexual acts, it is a fact of life that goes on, and I believe I would tell him to supply condoms to inmates. Just by issuing condoms doesn't say that everyone should go out and have sex, because there are a lot of people that don't mess around. But it would save lives in prison and in the streets. Sex is being practiced at an alarming rate throughout the prison system. And if it is going to happen anyway, why not make it safe?

"And I would also tell him inmates are transmitting the disease rapidly among themselves and then allowed back into society to spread it even more. Think of the men who have it and make HIV babies. The reason that is happening is because inmates don't know they have it because they were not tested. And also there should be medical specialists that deal in infectious diseases and not just a medical doctor who gets all his information from pamphlets and books and seminars. A doctor treating HIV patients should work and have firsthand knowledge of dealing with the disease. That's what I would tell the Governor."

This interview frightened me, not because it threatened my moral beliefs or my conservative way of life, but because it threatened my very *life*. AIDS has bound us all to Toney, because the virus which is eating away at his immune system is also eating away at our ability to trust each other. We are becoming as unforgiving as the deadly disease itself.

We can no longer welcome the stranger, pardon infidelities, or excuse even our own indiscretions. Our nightmare of the hopelessly desperate AIDS carrier has forced us to live in a purgatory of doubt and distrust, limiting our lives to the certainty of condoms, blood tests, and our own fidelities.

Toney died of AIDS in 1994.

Chapter 12

Albert Brown: A Permanent Resident

Editors' Note

The author's interview with Albert Brown skillfully contrasts the old with the new. In the old days, prisoners lined up in an orderly rank and file for every daily routine. A sort of silent system was routinely enforced with sanctions that verged on corporal punishment. By contrast, the new prison today is a place of remarkable laxity, disorder, and anarchy.

Today's prison, which is supposed to be the bastion of the status quo and the hallmark of uniformity, is changing faster than one can possibly imagine. There are more inmates and more prisons than ever before. There are women guards, doctors, lawyers, gym coaches, and teachers working in prisons today. There are even children in prisons. What would an Old Head who has spent a lifetime of incarceration think of these rapid changes?

Every day when I rushed out of my cell on some busy agenda, I always passed an elderly black neighbor quietly and contentedly sweeping the range floor. The only reason I even noticed him was the steady routine of his life was in stark contrast to the fast-paced upheaval around him. He seemed so impervious to it all.

Then one day I observed him explaining to a much younger man how he would be willing to relieve him of his burden of doing time.

I sensed there was more to this very Old Head than met the eye, so I decided to interview him.

Albert Brown is a 74-year-old lifer who looks more like he's in his late fifties. He stands a tall six-foot-one and has a deep, strong voice that hints at a hearing problem. One of the most impressive things about Mr. Brown is his air of honesty, something you don't hear very much of in prison.

Listening to his observations about prison life past and present, I learned why Mr. Brown cares little about change and even less about the rest of the world. As I watched this man, it was hard to resist the feeling that I was looking at the face of my future. I shuddered at the possibility that he represented the natural conse-quences of a lifetime in prison.

When Mr. Brown first came to prison in 1945 at age 25, separate but equal was the law of the land in the relations between blacks and whites. It was a very different world when he started serving his life sentence in the now abandoned Eastern Penitentiary in Philadelphia, which was built in 1829. In 1958, he was transferred to Western Penitentiary, which opened in 1826. (Eastern and West-ern Penitentiaries were among the first prisons built in the world.) In 1962, he was transferred back to Eastern, where he got into a fight with a white man. To avoid trouble, he asked for a transfer to Graterford Penitentiary and arrived there in 1964.

Prison Then

"At nine o'clock a guy would blow a trumpet and all the lights would go off and it was time to sleep. At six o'clock they would blow that trumpet again and it was time to eat breakfast. You would have to hurry and line up to eat. You better not butt in line or go out of place like they do today. No sir, you couldn't do none of that back then. . . .

"Whites and blacks were segregated. We were completely apart. There were about eleven blocks and they were almost even blacks and whites. . . . I never went to other blocks so I don't know what happened in the white blocks. . . . I have to say everybody was treated the same, [except that] white guys always got the best jobs. . . . Everybody ate the same thing. Even the guards would eat what we ate. . . .

"No dayroom, no TV, no radio, or nothing. They gave you head-phones that plugged into the wall. There was no newspapers and you were lucky if you got over an hour of yard when you got yard. There was no gym equipment. Nothing like that. The only magazine they would let you have was the *Christian Science Monitor*. People could write, but it was censored going and coming. . . .

"They had a library you could go to sometimes in the afternoon, but they only had some old books. Plus I couldn't read too well then. Blacks worked on the blocks as janitors or in the kitchen. All labor jobs. . . .

"They had novelty shops then. Inmates made things and they were allowed to sell them. Some had a big business with people coming and picking up their things regular. Some people would work for others. But only whites were allowed to do this. Sometimes if you had the right connection you could work for a white guy and make some money. . . .

"I could barely read or write. I went to school, and it was inmates who taught me how to read and write. Inmates did almost every-thing back then. There were inmate nurses, clerks, and teachers. There was even an ex-inmate pharmacist. He had been pardoned. Only whites had these jobs. We did have one black that did machine work. But the rest of us did labor. I worked in the laundry. . . .

"In 1956, there was a riot in Western Penitentiary. The inmates took control of the prison for a few days. After they took the prison back, the governor hired a new commissioner to clean up things in the prisons. He made a lot of changes for the better. They hired two black guards for the first time. One of them quit and soon returned to prison as an inmate. He said he quit because he couldn't lock people up. He's still at Graterford today, I think. . . . In 1960-61, the commissioner ordered an end to segregation. The Warden at Grater-ford refused to integrate. They fired him and forced desegregation. There was a few fights after they desegregated but no big problems. People didn't like it but they lived with it. . . . Afterwards, it was inmates that kept the dining room segregated. I remember there were people written up for not wanting to sit with blacks or whites in the dining hall. . . . I can't really say whether desegregation made things better or worse. They are pretty fair now. If there is racism, it is the inmates, not the prison. . . .

"I remember in the '60s I watched them [try to] put double cells in Graterford for the first time. The commissioner was there and he looked at it and said it was too small for two people and made them move them all out. He changed a lot of things for the better. . . .

"I never knew how important *Gideon* [the landmark case of *Gideon v. Wainwright* that established an accused criminal's right to counsel] would be. Before then, people couldn't come near any law things. They'd get in real trouble if they even tried. . . ."

The Hole

"I was in the Hole at old Eastern. I got two slices of bread at nine o'clock and two slices at three o'clock. No lights. A half a blanket on a metal bed. . . . The Hole weren't no joke back then. No, sir, they didn't fuck around with you back then like they do now. If a guard writes you up, they'd lock you up right away in your cell and just tell you what you done wrong. Nothing complicated and official like you get now.

"After a few days in your cell, guards would come and get you out of your cell and take you to the Deputy's [Superintendent's] Office. You know, back in them days the Deputy ran the prison. He wasn't like a figurehead the way they are now. Anyway, if the Deputy wasn't available, the Major or Captain took his place.

"The guards would take you to a waiting room off the Deputy's Office. Then they'd make you stand facing the wall with your nose on that wall. And you'd better not take that nose off that wall if you knew what was good for you. Those guards had them big sticks back then and they'd use 'em. Quick!

"They'd let you stand like that for a while and then they would take you into the Deputy's Office. He'd be sitting down at his big desk in front of you. You'd be standing in front of him with the guards around you. He'd ask you why you done whatever they say you did. You'd say your piece and then he'd tell you what he was going to do with you.

"At that time there was four places they could send you if they wanted to punish you. One place was the punishment block where they put all of the real bad troublemakers. Men that was always fighting or getting into some kind of trouble. They'd keep a man in the punishment block for a long time. They put him there years before they let him out. It was a whole separate block where everyone stayed locked in their cell. They never came out. No commissary or nothing. They might let them have a smoke every once in a while and they'd feed them three full meals a day, but they didn't get much more.

"Another place was the Gallery which was the top range of one of the blocks. It was just like the punishment block except they'd only keep a man up there for no more than a year. Usually a few months or so.

"Then there was what they called the Klondike. It was the back part of one of the blocks. I was there a few times when I was at Eastern. They put me in a small cell and gave me half a thin blanket and I had to sleep on a steel bed with no mattress. There were no lights inside, but it wasn't cold. I got two slices of bread twice a day. There was a cold-water spigot in the cell so I had all the water I needed. Every 72 hours I got one full meal. I was in there a few times, but the most time I did in there was 15 days.

"Then there was what they called the Hole. I remember there was a guy they say cursed at the Deputy. They put him in the Hole for four days. Then they took him to the Deputy and they say he cursed at him again, so they put him back in the Hole for 30 days. When they took him to the Deputy again, they say he acted up again. But they figured he was crazy and so they just let him alone after that. The Hole was a four-by-four-by-four-foot cell with a solid door they kept shut. You couldn't stand up or lay down all the way. You'd get bread and water in there with a full meal every three days. No sir, that Hole was no joke."

Prison Today

"The food changed a lot. It got a lot better. When I first came to prison we ate everything out of one bowl. They didn't have no trays like they do now. We would go through the line with our bowl and utensils and they would put all the food into the bowl. Everything went into that bowl. It took me about 11 years before I got used to the food. But [in the 1960s] things got better, everything got better. You got chicken and beef. They didn't have none of that [before]. . . .

"They treat you a lot better now. They have better medical care with real doctors and nurses. Inmates used to do all that. They have medication. I remember all they would give you was Epsom Salts for everything. They have college and schools now with teachers.

They didn't have none of that. . . . It's a lot better now. It's more human. . . .

"What makes me happy? Truthfully? If I could get a couple of Snickers Bars tonight and go to bed full and not hungry—I'm happy. Before they let you buy commissary in prison, I used to go to sleep hungry. Now with commissary and the 18 cents an hour I make, I'm happy. . . ."

Mr. Brown refuses to apply for parole, even though he has been eligible for many years. He has decided to remain a permanent resident of the Department of Corrections. Ironically, the cruelest thing the prison system could do to this man would be to release him into a society where he can no longer survive.

There are many more people like Mr. Brown in institutions throughout the country: spiritless, frightened souls who are quietly waiting to die in the only environment they feel comfortable in. These people represent a growing underclass of dependents in a world of change.

If this doesn't disturb you, maybe it should. Our system has become expert at making people forget about ever being free. If that doesn't bother you, then Mr. Brown wishes to thank you for being generous enough to pay the twenty-thousand dollars a year it takes to keep him where he wants to be.

Chapter 13

Jacko: Surviving the Hole

Editors' Note

In 1840, the superintendent of the Norfolk Island penal colony, Alexander Maconochie, invented a system of "grades" that still enjoys wide use in American prisons. A typical system uses three grades. For any serious infraction, a prisoner is sentenced to solitary confinement for 30 days, with the first days spent in third-grade solitary—"the Hole." The solid door of the Hole closes out all light and sound. Meals consist of two slices of bread per day and water, with a full meal every third day. After six days of good behavior, the prisoner graduates to second-grade solitary, where the barred door provides light and sound; three full meals are served daily, but no smoking or reading materials are allowed. After nine days of good behavior, the prisoner is then given first-grade solitary, where he has full access to smoking and reading materials. After 15 days of good behavior, the prisoner may be released back into the general population.

Hassine begins his interview of Jacko with a short description of the Pennsylvania system. What both refer to as the Hole is actually first-grade solitary confinement. Pennsylvania has abolished the use of third- or second-grade solitary confinement. Does this make the Pennsylvania system any more humane than the graded systems used in other states? Hassine thinks not; he argues that resourceful prison staff have devised ways to make even first-grade solitary confinement painful. The following interview demonstrates this point.

While prison is punishment for those who have violated society's laws, the Hole is punishment for those who have violated a prison's rules. The Hole represents a penal institution's harshest form of legalized punishment short of the death penalty. On the one hand, a prison always feeds an inmate to keep him strong and healthy; on the other, it develops and imposes new and more creative forms of punishment that seem to defy all standards of human decency.

When Mr. Brown recalled the Hole between the years of 1945 and 1955, he was describing the beginning of a twisted path which found its way to me some 35 years later. While the nature of punishment in prison seems to have changed, its intensity certainly has not.

In the 1950s, the Governor of Pennsylvania assigned the new Commissioner of Corrections the task of reforming the prison system. One of the things the new Commissioner changed was the way inmates were punished. The four-by-four-by-four-foot punishment cell described by Mr. Brown could no longer be used. Furthermore, it was required that inmates in solitary confinement be given three full meals per day and allowed exercise periods out of their cell. Corporal punishment was prohibited.

These profound changes generated a lot of resentment from prison employees, who felt unruly inmates were not being adequately punished. In response, what solitary confinement lost in severity it gained in total confinement time. Inmates who broke the rules were now sent to the Hole for much longer periods of time—in many cases, years at a time.

Other changes required that lights be provided for the men confined in solitary. In response to that, guards left bright, glaring lights shining in these isolated cells for 24 hours a day. One prison went so far as to build a cell out of transparent plexiglass, known as the "glass cage," in which unyieldingly bright lights glared down upon the exposed inmate.

Bright lights and more time were not the end to the backlash of post-reform punishments. Whenever possible, the cells in solitary were kept either shivering cold in the winter or stifling hot in the summer. Those three full meals a day were often served cold and in the most cruel manner. And, while corporal punishment was prohibited, "goon squads" were formed by the guards to administer

unofficial physical punishment. These goon squads were often comprised of guards who were not assigned to the general population,
so inmates could not recognize them. They never wore name tags
and their activities were never reported, at least not by the staff.

Thus, despite all the reforms, deprivation and physical force
remained the peacemaker at Graterford and other Pennsylvania
prisons. While it was true that inmates in solitary were now fed
three meals per day, given exercise time, and allowed lights in their
cell, the degree of cruelty remained the same or was more severe
than it had been in the past.

In fact, conditions in the punishment units of Pennsylvania's
prisons became such an outrage that in 1973 the Bureau of Corrections was faced with a court-ordered Consent Decree resulting from
a class-action suit, *Incarcerated Citizens Union (ICU) v. Shapp*, filed in
Federal District Court to challenge conditions in the state's solitary-
confinement cells. The Court had decided to try to institute and
enforce the reforms that the first Commissioner had attempted in
the 1950s. The ICU Consent Decree once again significantly changed
the way Pennsylvania punished its inmates.

In this interview with a fellow inmate, Jacko describes the Hole
at Graterford from 1976 to 1978. He recalls a much different place
than Mr. Brown's Klondike at old Eastern Penitentiary.

"I stayed in the Hole back then and, to tell you the truth, it wasn't
really too bad. They would call you over to the Day Captain's Office
and give you a misconduct report. Then you would go about your
business. Unless it was a real serious misconduct, like hitting a
guard or something, they never locked a man up until after the
misconduct hearing.

"A few days later you would get a pass to the old phone room
which was off of the main corridor right across from the laundry.
There was always a lot of people sitting on the benches in the
waiting room of the Hearing Room who were waiting for their
hearing. The room was small and stayed hot because there were no
windows and a whole lot of people. You'd sit there for hours sometimes until a guard from the Hearing Room would come out and call
your number.

"Once you finally got inside the Hearing Room, a guard would
pat you down and tell you to sit down in a chair that was right in
front of a big table. Sitting on the other side of the table was the

Major, a counselor, and a work supervisor. If the Major wasn't there, it would be a Captain or another white shirt [officer]. One of them would read the misconduct to you and ask you how you wanted to plead.

"At this time, you got a chance to say whatever you wanted to and then the guard would ask you to step outside. You always got found guilty, so basically all you were doing was waiting to see what punishment they were going to give you. You'd sit in the waiting room for a little while more until the guard would call you back in the Hearing Room. He would pat you down again and make you sit down in the same chair. Then the Major or one of the other guys would tell you what you got.

"They didn't really have cell restriction, loss of privileges, or any of that stuff back then. If they didn't send you to the Hole, they put you on probation or put you on the Gallery. Probation was when they would warn you that, if you got another misconduct any time soon, you would go to the Hole. That was it.

"The Gallery was the back half [50 cells] of the top range of B-Block on the A-Block side. If they sent you there, you went right from the hearing. But once you got to your cell in the Gallery, you could give the guard a list of things that he would bring to you from your cell. You could even have a TV and radio in the Gallery, and you also got commissary once a week.

"The section of B-Block where the Gallery was at had a steel mesh screen running along the outside of the top tier walkway, which separated it from the rest of the block. But you could still see and holler down to your friends in general population on B-Block. It got pretty noisy at times, but the guards didn't really mess with you about that. For recreation, you went to a small yard area between A- and B-Block two hours a day and they brought food to you off the main line three times a day.

"If you went to the Hole, you went right to Siberia. That was a whole separate building out by the wall on the opposite side of the cell blocks. The official name was the Behavioral Adjustment Unit [BAU]. We'd call it Bad Actors University.

"When you went to Siberia, you didn't take anything with you. You got the same meals and yard time as in the Gallery, but that was about it. Plus the guards kept it real cold in there. And if you made a lot of noise, they'd tell you to be quiet. If you didn't stop, the goon squad rushed you and beat your ass. That kept things pretty quiet.

"But to tell you the truth, I didn't mind the Hole, because they would give me all the medication I asked for. I mean I got Valium and Darvons—all I wanted. I stayed high. And as long as you didn't mess with the guards, they pretty much left you alone. But it was cold."

In addition to the improved conditions in what was now called "Punitive Segregation," Jacko was afforded the right to appeal his misconduct to a Program Review Committee and then to the Superintendent. If the Superintendent would not give him the relief he asked for, he could take his appeal up to the Commissioner. When Mr. Brown went to the Hole decades before, however, all he could do was his time.

The ICU Consent Decree also brought about a limit to the amount of time a Hearing Committee could confine a man in Punitive Segregation: a maximum of 180 days in the BAU or Gallery for every misconduct report. In response to this, guards who had previously listed all of an inmate's infractions on one misconduct report now issued separate misconduct reports for every infraction. In this way, the Hearing Committee could continue its practice of sending troublemakers to the Hole for years at a time.

This rush to fill the Hole with long-term residents resulted in a long-term shortage of cells in the Gallery and BAU (now renamed the "Restrictive Housing Unit," or RHU). By the time I faced my first misconduct hearing in 1982 for the hamburger caper, the Gallery had been expanded to double its former capacity. Furthermore, part of the RHU was double-celled, so that solitary confinement at Graterford was not so solitary anymore.

Aggravating the problem was the violence at Graterford, which had caused a dramatic increase in the number of inmates seeking protective custody, or self-lockup. For a multitude of reasons, these men could not be protected in general population, so they chose to live in the safety of solitary confinement. By housing them on the Gallery, the prison administration imposed on them the same restrictions used for many of the men who were serving punitive-segregation time. Unfortunately, as the violence escalated, these restrictions were not enough to stem the tide of inmates seeking protective custody.

Consequently, the Hearing Committee was no longer free to punish misbehaving inmates by sending them to the RHU or the Gallery. There just weren't enough cells. So new sanctions were developed, one of which was the cell restriction I received for my burger infraction. Another was "double lock feed-in," which allowed an inmate to serve RHU time in his cell until such time as a cell in the RHU or the Gallery became available.

The nature and the effect of punishment at Graterford and other prisons are still in flux. In my view, guards' resistance to reform, combined with overcrowding, have to this day prevented a reasonable system of punishment from being realized or evaluated. In fact, crisis management, along with a heavy dose of resentment and spite, seem to be resulting in an increase in the level of punishments.

One final thought about the Hole and other harsh punishments is that people adapt. If you throw a prisoner into a dark cave, he'll learn how to see. If you feed him rats, he'll still eat. In fact, if you give him enough rats, he'll get fat. You can try feeding him cockroaches to punish him more, but he'll eventually get fat on those, too. As inmates sometimes boast, "What doesn't kill me only makes me stronger." Once you start down the road toward ruthless punishments, there's no turning back.

Chapter 14

Coach: A Changeling

Editors' Note

A famous social psychological experiment conducted at Stanford University in the early 1970s tried to simulate the conditions of imprisonment by randomly dividing two dozen male college student volunteers into a group of prisoners and a group of guards. When brought to the mock prison (located in the basement of the psychology building), prisoners were stripped, deloused, dressed in a uniform, and put into a cell with two other inmates; guards wore khaki shirts and pants and were equipped with wooden batons and reflecting sunglasses that made eye contact impossible. The researchers intended to observe how normal men would adjust to these roles and the conditions of incarceration for two weeks.

The study was abandoned after only six days because the behavior of the subjects quickly deteriorated. Almost overnight, average young men were transformed into either servile, depressed, and withdrawn prisoners or tyrannical, brutal, and conspiratorial guards. The researchers concluded that the "pathology of imprisonment" led to these rapid personality changes.

Scholars still dispute whether corruption and brutality among guards is largely the product of conditions inside prisons or is caused by outside influences that predate correctional work. The Stanford prison experiment suggests the former; so does Hassine in his interview with Coach. Discerning readers of this selection, however, will find evidence on both sides of the argument.

It has been my experience that violence—inside *and* outside of prison—is learned behavior. Even the gentlest person in the world will discover that he has to become violent after spending five years in a prison like Graterford. He will learn violence not because of shame, not because of some personal slight, but because that's the way business is done in this part of town.

What goes for prisoners also goes for prison staff. Logic dictates that if overcrowded, violent, and understaffed prisons teach rage, violence, and criminality to prisoners, then these conditions inevitably will affect staff members, who spend a significant amount of their waking hours in the same environment.

Recently I read a newspaper report about three inmates who were savagely beaten by a group of corrections officers in a particularly overcrowded county prison in Pennsylvania. The three inmates had each struck a corrections officer in separate, unrelated incidents. These incidents resulted in retaliation by a mob of angry corrections officers, beating and kicking the three inmates with batons, fists, and boots *after* the inmates had been subdued, placed in handcuffs, and secured in isolation cells.

Eventually a nurse and a corrections officer were persuaded to come forward and give eyewitness accounts of the incident. The nurse described how one inmate had been beaten so badly that when prison guards brought him to her for medical treatment, his body resembled a "Frankenstein" monster. The nurse also recalled how she had heard the pleadings of the inmate during the beating. Despite having witnessed this horrifying incident, the nurse stated that she had not immediately reported the event because she feared the loss of her job and the retaliation of the same officers, whose job it was to protect her whenever she worked in the prison.

During the course of a subsequent federal investigation into the beatings, several corrections officers decided to plead guilty for their parts in the crime and also agreed to testify against other officers who participated in the beatings. In April of 1997, four corrections officers were tried in a Federal District Court for the beatings of the three inmates.

"I became almost blind with rage when these incidents happened," testified one of the cooperating corrections officers. "I just got out of hand." When he was asked why he reacted the way he did, the prison guard answered, "I think I would need a psychiatrist to figure that out." And when he was asked if he later received mental health treatment, he responded, "The best treatment I got was getting out of there."

The remorseful prison guard went on to describe how during one of the beatings a Lieutenant had scolded him for not using two hands to strike a helpless inmate with a baton. The Lieutenant, who ". . . seemed like he was showing off . . . ," just began ". . . flailing away . . ." at the inmate with a series of two-handed baton blows.

When an attorney for one of the accused corrections officers defended his client by suggesting that beating inmates who struck prison guards was the only way to maintain order in prison, a cooperating officer firmly disagreed. "I thought at the time it was necessary. That's the thinking I had. My thinking now is [that] you have to have people in there who are suitable. . . . The inmates aren't perfect. But then, neither are the guards."

Another cooperating officer testified at the trial that he participated in the beatings because he was just ". . . trying to fit in with fellow officers." A third cooperating guard explained that he kept quiet about the incident because he didn't want to be labeled a "snitch."

The brutality of the corrections officers—their inmate-like behavior, conspiratorial silence, fear, and rage—suggests that they became morally depraved by working in prison. Something altered their understanding of right and wrong. Something made them as perverse as the men they guarded and despised—perhaps even more so. As a result of their working environment, they had become mentally unfit.

One example of this mysterious personality change is a man who answers to the prison handle "Coach." Coach is currently serving prison time for robbery and rape. Before becoming an inmate, he was a big-city police officer and a corrections officer. Coach's journey helps us to understand the process that changes the jailer into the jailed.

"I grew up [in Philadelphia in the 1940s and 1950s]. I had a good childhood considering the racism and discrimination that existed at the time. That was the heyday of the gang era, and I was a gang leader and had a well-known reputation in our neighborhood of being from a family where everyone knew how to fight. In some respects, my childhood upbringing had a lot to do with my adult behavior before getting into trouble. I learned to share and care for others early in life because I came from a large family. I learned to be accountable for my actions and [I learned] a sense of responsibility from taking care of and protecting my younger sisters.

"My father died while I was very young. My mother raised me and my . . . brothers and sisters by doing housework as well as [from] my father's Social Security survivors' benefits. I can remember every holiday we would get together with my aunts, uncles, and other family for dinners at our house. . . .

"My father had been a boxer and, as a result, all of my brothers would try out boxing. . . . We were a close-knit family. To this day I have a very close relationship with my siblings. . . .

"Actually, although I didn't get a high school diploma until I got out of the Army, I had been an A student in elementary school and middle school. I dropped out of school for no reason other than to have more time to hang out in the streets. Eventually I met the woman (then a girl) who I would later marry. She became pregnant, and I knew that I would have to do something with my life. That's when I went into the Army.

"After getting out of the Army, I took the civil service test for the post office. I was hired within 90 days. I worked for the post office for five years and it was during this time I went back to school. I got my GED and went on to take college courses. . . . I left the post office and became . . . a police officer. This was during the late '60s and early '70s, a time of great strife when civil rights workers were becoming active.

"I left the police force but I retained my police commission and became a bail enforcement officer—a bounty hunter—for a bail bonding agency. It was then that I decided to become a corrections officer. I worked for both the Philadelphia prison system and the Pennsylvania Department of Corrections. My goal was to become a criminal psychoanalyst or a counselor. I was working toward that goal by taking college courses in those fields.

"In 1974, I became a state corrections officer at Graterford. I preferred corrections over police work because, as a cop, my only contact with offenders was to arrest them. That was it. My college courses were in the behavioral sciences, psychology and sociology, which gave me a desire to get to know and possibly be of some assistance to the offenders. As a police officer, I knew that I couldn't do that, but also as a corrections officer I found that it was hard to do. I was always chided by other officers for being too much of a social worker. I left Graterford in 1981 and went into the Philadelphia county prison system until 1985.

"There has always been a lot of racism in law enforcement [and] corrections work, . . . which often got me into trouble at Graterford. In Holmesburg [a Philadelphia County prison], it wasn't a problem since most of the guards and supervisors were black. My relationship with inmates has always been good no matter where I worked. Many of the C.O.s wanted to see inmates treated like trash; they expected all C.O.s to act the same. But all of us didn't feel that way.

"When I worked at Graterford, it was a very dangerous and violent jail. Corruption was everywhere. During my tenure, I had a take in the gambling games that were run on A-Block. I knew guards were pimping the homos and selling weed and drugs. Graterford was still better than Holmesburg. There was a lot of money to be made. White Hats [high-ranking corrections officials] were in on it as well.

"I saw so many instances of abuse and cruel treatment of inmates that, for the most part, I would disassociate myself from it. There were a few times when I subjected an unruly inmate to my own private brand of cruel treatment, like an ass-whooping, up close and personal. But I never rushed an inmate with a gang of guards. I saw many incidents of guards putting shanks [prison knives] in inmates' mattresses and then come back to shake them down, beat 'em up and write 'em up [issue a misconduct citation].

"Over the years I have cut down inmates who hung up [tried to commit suicide]. Sometimes I saved their lives. Sometimes they were dead when I found them. I saw one inmate get his throat cut wide open over his commissary at Graterford. He was dead by the time he got to the hospital.

"[I once saw an inmate] . . . punch a guard in the face in the dining hall at Graterford. . . . The guard fell and hit his head on . . . [a] table and was killed. There was a minor riot in the D-Block kitchen. Once we quelled it, [the inmate] was placed in the Hole. He was charged with murder.

"While he waited for trial, he was kept at Graterford instead of being moved to another institution. He was kept naked in his cell [in Siberia] without blankets or sheets. He was hosed down with cold water every time he tried to sleep. Eventually he came down with a very bad viral infection and died in the infirmary.

"Another incident that sticks out in my mind was when [another officer] was killed . . . in the main corridor of Graterford. I was working the door on D-Block corridor. The men from the yard were coming in and [the officer was standing there]. . . . [An inmate] came in with a [baseball] bat and the officer stopped him, verbally chastised him, and told him to return the bat to the yard. . . . [As the officer] turned to walk away, [the inmate] . . . hit him in the back of the head with the bat.

"A crowd of inmates was blocking the view, so me and some other guards went to see what was going on. . . . [The officer's] head was smashed in. There was a big puddle of brains and blood. . . .

"[Several years later] . . . I was the officer in charge of . . . [protective custody] in another Philadelphia County prison. . . . While in my charge, [one] inmate got into a fight with another inmate and was beaten in the head with a mop wringer. [The inmate] . . . was injured very badly and later died. I was charged with negligence for allowing that to happen, and I was suspended and fired. I was unemployed with a new home, new car, plus a wife and kids; economically I was strapped. Eventually, I took my retirement funds, bought a large amount of cocaine, and became a drug dealer. Soon I became the leader of a large organized drug ring, which led me to be charged with a variety of crimes. I took a deal for a guilty plea and . . . [was sent to prison].

"I have run into a lot of inmates who knew me when I was a guard. No one has shown me any resentment. If they did, it was behind my back. I've never had a problem since I've been down. It was very humiliating after being a C.O. for so long and then being a convicted felon. The guards have always treated me well. My block card is marked so the guards know who I am.

"Prison hasn't helped me. I think I am a better person for coming to prison, but not for being in prison, if you know what I mean. . . ."

When you consider the atrocities that Coach witnessed while he was trying to "be of some assistance to the offenders," his later crimes seem predictable. Certainly the corruption, hostility, violence, and criminality in his workplace must bear some blame for Coach's fall from grace.

Because I have lived for so long in prison, I understand the perversity that transforms inmates and staff. A crucial ingredient in this metamorphosis is the daily hatred and disregard that staff express toward inmates, *and* that inmates express toward staff. Like carnival mirrors, captives and captors reflect, distort, and amplify each other's basest personality defects and worst behavioral deficiencies.

Some years ago, while Coach was working at Holmesburg, I was privileged to hear a survivor of the Nazi concentration camp at Auschwitz speak to the Jewish inmates at Graterford. Itka was her name, and she was a woman I will never forget. I knew that she had been deeply wounded by an experience much worse than mine, yet I never detected the unmistakable bitterness, hostility, and cynicism in her that binds the ignominious fraternity of prison inmates together like a secret handshake.

One of the inmates asked Itka how she felt about the Germans today. I could tell that he and most of the other men wanted to share in the bitter feast of her hatred. She responded by crossing the index and middle fingers of her right hand, like a child making a wish, and raised them over her head for all the men to see.

"When two people hate each other they become like my two fingers. No matter who is the stronger or the more powerful, each one is enslaved by his hatred of the other. The same way you cannot determine which of my crossed fingers subdues the other, two people joined by their hatred of each other cannot be free from the restraints they place on the other through their hatred, because the effort needed to hate is as oppressive as any act of malice."

Itka then displayed her fingers in the sign of a "V." "Even after I was liberated from Auschwitz, I was not truly free. Only when I stopped hating the Germans was I able to uncross my fingers and free myself from the bondage of those feelings that had kept us both captive. Today I come to you a free woman to tell you the secret to freedom: you have to stop hating."

It takes a courageous person like Itka to bury the hatred that seems to be the inevitable byproduct of the human warehouses called prisons. As a result, the construction of each new warehouse poses an immense harm to our moral landscape. Collectively, as politicians and citizens, victims and offenders, correctional officials and prisoners, we all now must be brave enough to uncross our fingers.

Chapter 15

The Dancing Man

Editors' Note

In the form of a self-interview, the author offers a vivid first-hand account of a prison riot. During this riot, Hassine witnessed what he claims has become his saddest memory during 17 years of incarceration: the repeated beating and gang rape of a young inmate taken from protective custody. The author sharply criticizes prison staff for videotaping the episode and not acting to stop the torture.

When I interview people for the pieces that I write, I begin by asking questions that spark memories of the major events that shaped their impressions of prison. I ask my interviewees what their happiest memory was during their incarceration, then what their saddest memory was, then what their angriest memory was, and so on. You can tell a lot by what a person chooses to remember, as well as by what he chooses to forget.

My saddest memory of prison is the dancing man. The experience taught me that death isn't the worst thing that can happen to you in prison. Living can be far worse: living in fear in protective custody; living as somebody's sex slave; living under somebody's thumb, helpless to do anything about it.

During the fall of 1986, I was transferred from Graterford to SCI-Pittsburgh (Western Penitentiary). An inmate at Graterford had attacked me for no apparent reason. To me, it was just another act of random violence at Dodge City, but to the prison administration, it offered a good excuse to get rid of me.

A prison transfer is much more than just a move from one place to another. It is more like moving from one country to another, because all prisons are unique. The rules are different, the guards are different, the inmates are different, even the food is different. This particular transfer took me far away from my loved ones. At Graterford, my family in Trenton, New Jersey, was only two and a half hours away. Now here I was in Pittsburgh, seven hours away by car. Visits became sporadic.

The move devastated and embittered me. I felt isolated, victimized, and alone. To make matters worse, I was now in a badly overcrowded prison. Graterford was single-celled when I left, but inmates in SCI-Pittsburgh were double-celled. Furthermore, Pittsburgh's inmate population (about 2,200 men) was only slightly smaller than Graterford's, but the prison was so small that you could almost fit its entire physical structure into Graterford's main yard.

In the early morning hours of a very cold October day soon after I arrived at Western Penitentiary, I was awakened by the smell of smoke and cries of "Fire! Fire!" A guard, covering his mouth and nose with a wet cloth, opened my cell with one free hand and quickly moved down the range, opening other cells that were out of sight. The smoke was thick and the confusion grew as startled inmates ran from their cells. I stayed in my cell until I was dressed, putting on my heaviest boots and several layers of shirts and pants. Remembering a lesson I had learned at Graterford, I stuffed a thick stack of old newspapers against my chest and my back as protection from a possible knife attack. Finally, I took my gloves, a lighter, and a few packs of cigarettes.

When I finished dressing, I carefully pushed my belongings out of sight under my bed, turned out the light, and then locked my cell with a padlock. For a moment, I stood motionless on the range to watch what was happening. Suddenly, the guard who had unlocked my door came running past me, heading down a flight of stairs and off the cellblock, but not before he dropped a set of block keys on the floor a few feet away from me. I could hear men above me yelling, "Let me out, C.O.! Let me out!" As I eyed the keys, I wondered if I should risk danger to release the hundreds of men trapped on the upper tiers of the block. However, another inmate picked up the keys and began unlocking the cells. Just in case his bravery turned into larceny, I decided to check to make sure the padlock was secure on my cell.

The smoke thickened, but because I was on the second of five levels, I could still breathe and see. Looking up the tiers, I saw no flames, just a thick, black cloud of smoke floating downward.

The sound of inmates screaming and running down steel stairs probably would frighten most people, but I was a veteran of three riots at Graterford, so smoke, disorder, and noise didn't scare me. I cautiously headed toward the ground floor of the cellblock, trying to discern if I was witnessing a fire or a riot.

During times of confusion in prison, it is wise to travel with a pack, in case things get ugly. But I had only been in Pittsburgh for a month, so I didn't know many people. My only alternative was to walk slowly and deliberately to a place where my back was protected, where I had a clear, unobstructed view of the unfolding events. When I got to the "flats" (what inmates call the ground floor of a cellblock), I went to a brightly lit area next to the exit door, keeping my back to the wall. In the mounting chaos, I became a proverbial fly on the wall that nobody noticed.

I soon realized that I was looking at a fire, not a riot. A subsequent investigation revealed that an unknown guard on the graveyard shift had gone into the basement of the block, deliberately setting the fire next to several giant ventilation fans. The massive air ducts located on the ceiling of the five-story cellblock spewed out the thick, black smoke from the basement, choking inmates locked in their cells on the top tiers. No one ever discovered who that guard was or why he or she set the fire.

Because no one knew yet that there was smoke but no real fire, inmates were carrying armloads of belongings from their cells. Men with TVs, radios, and typewriters streamed out into the ranges. I could see inmates on the upper tiers covering their faces with wet rags, going from cell to cell to make sure that no one was locked inside. I stayed to watch the pandemonium, because I was in no mood to brave the wind and the cold outside.

After about 30 minutes of general chaos and confusion, things gradually turned ugly. By this time most inmates realized that the smoke was coming from the air ducts and there was no immediate danger from a real fire, so men began returning to the block to escape the cold and to keep an eye on their possessions. Right in front of me, a gang of about 10 hooded men who had been roaming through the ranges tried to throw someone over the third tier to his certain death. For the first time, I could see flames in the back of the block from inmates setting cell fires. I knew that this chaos was quickly turning into a riot.

A small inmate who walked by was suddenly attacked from behind by two men, who beat him to the ground and kicked him. A third man soon appeared, who grabbed the small inmate by the hair and dragged him to a cell off the flats. I knew what fate awaited the small man. About this time, ten inmates carrying metal rods began to hammer at the steel mesh fence that surrounded 50 cells in the adjacent protective custody unit. I could see two guards nervously pacing up and down the unit, calling for help on their hand-held, two-way radios.

The steel mesh gates finally collapsed, and a mob of 20 or more inmates rushed inside the unit. The two guards were beaten, kicked, and clubbed. Once the guards stopped struggling, the inmates spat on them and urinated on them, only to begin beating them again. Eventually, the guards were stripped and dragged into empty, unlit cells. Several inmates took the guards' keys and began to unlock the protective custody cells.

The two guards had been out of my view for several minutes when one captain and two city police officers (I think one was a woman) came into the block. Amazingly, the riotous frenzy stopped in its tracks. Maybe it was the fear of uniformed authority, or possibly no one was certain whether the officers were armed, but the three rescued the two injured guards without any resistance. Only the fear of brute force prompted the inmates' humanitarianism.

After the five officers left the block, the mob became far more enraged and violent, probably because they realized they hadn't mustered the courage needed to attack the rescuers. Inmates now fell upon the men who had been confined to protective custody with unbridled savagery and ferocity. I finally walked out of the building from sheer disgust. As I exited, I saw several inmates carrying a blonde-haired, blue-eyed youngster over their heads, away from isolation.

The sudden sting of frigid air on my face restored my senses. The thick stack of newspapers that I had stuffed into my shirt now protected me from the knife-like wind. I walked in relative warmth around the small prison yard, watching shivering men in bathrobes huddle in groups around the bonfires they had built. Graterford had taught me well.

For an hour or so, I stayed outside. My block was now engulfed in flames, so all the men (over 600) had left the building. The police and prison staff had managed to maintain control of the entire prison, except for the yard, the burning cellblock, and the auditorium (a rectangular building next to the cellblock). There was an elevated corridor about 15 feet above the ground that connected the auditorium projection room with the administrative building.

Eventually, I decided to escape the bitter cold by taking my chances in the auditorium. Inside, there were a hundred or so men, which meant the building wasn't as crowded as it should have been. It was enclosed, dark, and out of the reach of the authorities, so it was very dangerous. But I was colder than I was frightened. Prison riots were becoming mostly a nuisance to me, so I cautiously entered this no man's land.

At first, I saw what I wanted to see: a cast-iron heating element against one wall. I inched toward the heater, carefully keeping my back to the wall. I leaned against that heater for several hours, trading immediate warmth for a lifetime of terrible memories, nightmares, and disillusionment.

It took a while for my eyes to adjust to the darkness, even though there were small fires of burning furniture scattered around the auditorium. Eventually, in the flickering light, I saw roving gangs of inmates attacking and beating each other. I saw a couple of men thrown into a bonfire. But what haunts me to this day was what was happening on the stage: a satanic performance at the gates of hell. A hole was torn open in the curtain of humanity that day.

The men who had carried the blonde youngster from protective custody had taken him to the auditorium. They had stripped him naked and were repeatedly beating him, forcing him to dance around the stage for his life. Between these dances, hooded inmates alone and in groups raped him, striking him time and again until he performed every imaginable sex act. Some of the inmates cut the young man, others urinated on him or shoved various objects in every opening in his body. When they weren't raping or beating him, they forced him to dance on and on, like a marionette on strings. For hours, he screamed and pleaded for mercy. He must have prayed for his own death.

What made this even worse was that the police were watching the scene from the safety of the projection room above the auditorium. They videotaped the atrocities that were performed on the stage, but they never tried to help the dancing man. They simply watched.

To me, the tragedy lies not only in the senseless fate of the young man but more so in the failure to stop his suffering. The police certainly could have done something; maybe I could have, too. At the time, the police recorded the incident on videotape; now I've recorded it years later on paper. Sometimes I see us all standing in that projection room, staff and inmates together, watching and condemning the brutality but without the moral indignation needed to stop the hideous music that compelled this man to dance. The sinner or the pitiless: who is worse?

These thoughts haunt me every day. I will never forget the dancing man looking up toward the projection room—and toward me—begging for someone's help. I should have stayed outdoors on that frigid October day because, as it turned out, it was far colder indoors.

PART III

Op Ed

Editors' Note

In this third section, Hassine presents several opinion essays which express his social-activist view of the prison system. Unlike the material presented in the first two sections, each of these op ed chapters are intended to argue a point. Whether readers agree or disagree with any of these arguments, the author offers his authentic perspective on some of the most pressing problems facing American prisons today.

Chapter 16

Prison Overcrowding

Editors' Note

Not long ago, criminologists debated whether society has a natural "capacity to punish." Interest in this question was motivated by the observation that while crime rates rose and fell over time, imprisonment rates had remained constant throughout history. In the late 1970s, however, imprisonment rates began to explode, refuting the empirical basis of this debate. While the causes of the population explosion are clear, the effects are yet to be discovered. When the full effects of overcrowding are finally examined, however, the effects on the quality of prison life will more than likely be excluded. For that reason alone, the author's accounting of these effects are of importance.

What Is Overcrowding?

Prison overcrowding is a much overused term to describe an aggregate of related conditions that plague prisons all over the country. Despite its overuse, it is seldom explained in graphic terms that students and lay people can fully grasp. Instead, it is depicted as a vague, generalized "social problem"—a euphemism for the extreme, hopeless, horrifying, and tragic conditions that truly exist. The blood and guts of what prison overcrowding is *inside* and what it really does to the insiders remains an enigma to most outsiders.

The thin but durable veneer of this euphemism was poignantly revealed to me by a fellow inmate as we sat on the crowded bleachers of a crowded yard in a very overcrowded prison. After reading

129

a newspaper article on the topic, he spat a plug of tobacco on the ground, turned to me, and said: "These people keep blaming everything in here on overcrowding. It's overcrowding this and overcrowding that. Well, who the hell *is* this guy that's overcrowding us, anyway? And, if they know he's causing all these problems, why the hell don't they lock his ass up?"

His comment was more than just an angry sarcasm. It suggested some fundamental questions: What *is* prison overcrowding? What impact does overcrowding have on the experience of imprisonment?

First Came Crowded

As the term implies, prisons must have been crowded before they became overcrowded. Crowding in prisons was planned; overcrowding was not. Since the early 1800s when penitentiaries were first built, the one aspect of prison design that has survived is the practice of housing as many inmates as possible in the smallest cells possible, while meeting their minimal needs using a minimum of staff.

When I first came to Graterford, I entered a very crowded place supported by a very controlled, structured system designed to confine a mass of inmates, yet provide for them in the most economical way. Years of prison riots, reform, trial and error, design innovations, common sense, and just plain luck have brought about an evolution of prisons into a system of 1,700 men responding to klaxon bells, obeying orders, and traveling in unison down a tried and true maze of day-to-day prison existence.

Then Came Overcrowded

With the arrival of that "guy" who was overcrowding us, suddenly nothing worked right. Our lives became a daily challenge to avoid injury and stay out of trouble, which left us little time to reflect on the errors of our ways. In essence, the penitentiary evolved into a ghetto.

Once its prison population exceeded design capacity, Graterford became overcrowded. This numerical imbalance forced officials to institute double-celling or barracks-styled housing in order to accommodate the surplus population, despite the fact that the prison's cell blocks were not built for that kind of traffic.

While much can be argued about the psychological and physical dangers of squeezing two men into a poorly lit, poorly ventilated, bathroom-sized cell, the true evil of overcrowding has very little to do with crowded living space. Human beings, if they must, can and have lived in caves and tunnels. The destructive nature of prison overcrowding stems from the fact that it came unplanned, and was imposed on a system specifically created to discourage the confinement of too many inmates in one place.

Suddenly we inmates found ourselves at odds with our own rigidly designed environment. Furthermore, while inmate populations skyrocketed, the hiring of staff to support them did not increase proportionately. In Graterford and in many other prisons, the hiring of treatment staff (e.g., teachers, counselors, and vocational instructors) was in fact frozen—while an endless number of illiterate and needy inmates stormed the prison gates.

Overcrowding as a Personal Experience

As an inmate confined to one Pennsylvania prison or another since 1981, I have experienced what overcrowding has done, is doing, and threatens to do. By the mid-1980s, I was fairly well dug into my prison routine, working, obeying, and vegetating. I had a single cell, and for better or worse the prison system was functioning at an adequate level.

Then one day, my cell door opened and another man was shoved inside. My world was suddenly turned upside-down.

My first argument with my new co-tenant was, of course, over who got the top or bottom bunk. Then we fought over lights on or lights off, hygiene habits, toilet-use etiquette, cell cleaning, property storage, and whose friends could visit. Then there was missing property, accusations of thievery, snoring, farting, and smoking. As these arguments raged on every day, new ones would arise to make things worse.

Since the prison staff was somewhat taken by surprise by this sudden overpopulation, there was no time to plan or screen double-celling. Inmates were shoved together solely on the basis of race, age, or cell availability. Nor did an inmate have any opportunity to screen potential cellmates. If you didn't voluntarily find someone to move in with you, one would be picked for you at random. This practice immensely compounded the problems associated with double-celling. It was bad enough living with a stranger in such close quarters without having to worry about whether he was a Jeffrey Dahmer.

As my day-to-day struggle with my cellmate became a fact of life, I realized just how much this guy Mr. Overcrowding was causing me serious problems in every aspect of my prison life. As the next chapter shows, the possibility of one day waking up to a cannibal beside me, while certainly a cause for alarm, proved to be the least of my concerns.

Chapter 17

Prison Rape

Editors' Note

Prison rape is arguably the most sordid aspect of incarceration today. Because prison administrators, victims, and offenders are reluctant to discuss the topic, little is known about its true nature and extent. Although most scholars believe that rape is fairly common in men's medium- and maximum-security prisons, what we know about the topic is based mostly on hearsay reports and gossip among inmates along the "jailhouse grapevine." This makes Hassine's remarks and opinions regarding the causes, consequences, and types of prison rape indispensable.

While correctional insiders might dispute a few of the author's conclusions those who are honest must acknowledge that Hassine's comments are candid and generally accurate. Readers less familiar with prisons may be shocked and disgusted by his forthright descriptions of "pitching" and "catching," inmate-on-inmate "strong-arm" rape, and staff-on-inmate "surrogate" rape. Given the pivotal symbolism of rape in the "mind-games" played in men's prisons—where inmates endlessly struggle for dominance, constantly testing each other's weaknesses—it is unlikely that even the most conscientious prison administrators could stop some of these assaults.

Rape is no longer a random act of violence that occurs occasionally in prison: it is now a common event behind bars. Few inmates today are free from the fear of rape. The strong and the weak, gang members and loners, cautious inmates and reckless ones all are potential victims of violent, uninhibited inmates in violent, overcrowded prisons. Sexual assaults are so pervasive in correctional facilities today that they have become unspoken, *de facto* parts of court-imposed punishments.

The culprit behind the explosion of prison rape is prison overcrowding. With overcrowding, prison rape has evolved from an unspeakable act of depraved violence into a key strategy in the fight for dominance, complete with its own sophisticated techniques. In the process, prison rapists have been elevated from the status of degenerates into shrewd predators admired for their tactics.

The Rise in Prison Rape

Since the late 1970s, the nationwide prison population has more than tripled. (In Pennsylvania the population has more than quadrupled.) Prison managers have faced the immediate concerns of housing, clothing, and feeding the flood of men, women, and even children who were suddenly being sent to prison. Meeting these basic human needs continues to be a daily challenge for prison administrators, who find themselves without the necessary resources to maintain adequate living conditions, let alone to protect inmates from each other.

In an effort to reduce the skyrocketing costs of operating overcrowded prisons, state legislatures have imposed fiscal restraints on prison spending, often including hiring freezes. As a result, the inmate-to-staff ratio in most prisons has increased. This reduction in prison employee hiring has significantly contributed to the increase in violence that now plagues many prisons.

Administrators found themselves forced to implement untested inmate management practices and procedures to deal with overcrowding. One of the most significant and disastrous of the new policies was the practice of putting two or more inmates in a prison cell specifically designed for single occupancy.

But even with double-celling, administrators could not meet the confinement needs of an ever-growing prison population. As a result, recreation areas, such as gymnasiums and day rooms, were converted into dormitories for the barracks-style housing of inmates. Once called "temporary" or "emergency" measures, double-celling and dormitory housing have lasted for so long that they have become standard prison practices.

The reluctance of prison managers to abandon the practice of double-celling and dormitory housing does not entirely come out of necessity. In the short run, these emergency measures greatly reduced per-inmate housing costs. If it cost $20,000 a year to confine a single person in a single prison cell, confining two people in the same cell could cut costs almost in half. In the long run, though, these savings might be illusory. Double-celling and dormitory housing breed violence, disease, and lawsuits, drastically increasing prison medical and legal costs.

Once the decision to double-cell was made, prison managers began to develop practical means to determine which inmates would be confined together. Again, pressure compelled administrators to take "temporary, emergency" measures that overlooked the long-term consequences of their actions. This time the order went out for inmates to find their own cellmates. Those inmates who failed to find a cellmate were randomly double-celled. If an inmate refused to double-cell, he was taken to the Hole until he consented.

Administrators never considered how these policies could become a boon to prison rapists. Sexual predators inadvertently were allowed to pick their victims and to rape them in the privacy of their own cells! Once he "turned-out" his victim (slang for getting the victim to submit to his fate as a jailhouse whore), the rapist was free to find a new cellmate to attack. Administrators are helpless to stop prison rapists because it is too costly to hire enough staff to watch each double-cell and dormitory bunk.

The problem is compounded because victims of rape are reluctant to report the crime to authorities. This silence spares cost-conscious prison officials the expense and the burden of investigating and prosecuting incidents of prison rape. Rapists are thus virtually handed licenses for their attacks.

Recent inmate employment policies have compounded these problems. Before overcrowding, every able-bodied inmate was required to work. But when prison administrators found themselves with more inmates than available jobs, the policy of total inmate employment was modified. Current prison policy defines inmate work as a privilege that only the deserving are entitled to receive. A large percentage of inmates have been left idle and impoverished as a result of this new employment policy. The practical consequence is the creation of a large underclass of unemployed and desperate inmates, who engage in endless mischief in order to generate income and keep busy.

Prison violence, and especially rape, thrive in this climate of chronic double-celling, dormitory housing, unemployment, lax security, and poor management. In prisons today, rapists have their free pick of victims.

The New Views of Staff and Inmates

It appears that prison staff members have recently relaxed their attitudes about the rape of inmates. Some staff members now seem to view prison rape as a part of the punishment-risk that lawbreakers take when they commit their crimes. Others see it simply as retribution carried out on an interpersonal level.

Some officials view prison rape as a type of sexual gratification, in a violent environment where sex is usually denied. Others believe that one inmate raping another is simply a reflection of every inmate's moral depravity. Pragmatic prison officials probably see rape as an effective management tool that provides potentially dangerous inmates with sexual gratification, while at the same time pitting inmates against each other.

Whatever their beliefs, it is likely that the inability of prison staff to prevent rape has led to greater acceptance of the crime. Prison managers no longer consider the prevention of rape to be an important priority.

Among inmates, some interesting changes in prison slang suggest that views about rape have become more tolerant. The terms "pitchers" and "catchers" currently are used to refer to sex partners in prison. Because pitchers take on the "masculine" role by sodomizing other men, they consider themselves heterosexual. Derogatory names like homo, faggot, or queer now apply only to the "feminine" catchers (willing or unwilling victims of sexual predators). This change in prison slang not only protects the prison rapist/pitcher from the stigma of homosexuality, it also shows how the modern practice of prison rape has changed how inmates think.

I do not mean to imply that every new inmate in prison is going to be raped or become a rapist. Many men in prison today say that "whether a man pitches or catches, he is still playing ball," which means that they want to maintain a conventional heterosexual orientation, despite the pressures of prison life. (The primary release for these inmates is masturbation, still the most common sexual outlet in prison.) But it is true that prisoners are becoming the victims of prison rape in increasing numbers and that prison administrators appear to be unable or unwilling to bring an end to this kind of violence.

Victims Who Report Prison Rapes

Inmates who have been raped by other inmates seldom report these crimes, mostly because of the way they are treated by prison officials. Prisons are not designed to administer justice; the primary job of prison administrators is to maintain order and discipline while preventing escapes. Therefore, when a victim reports a rape to prison authorities, both the victim and the rapist will immediately be locked in isolation under different statuses (protective custody for the victim; disciplinary custody for the offender). Despite these different statuses, the victim and the offender get the same basic treatment.

Prison administrators very seldom initiate criminal prosecution against a rapist. Local prosecutors are reluctant to indict prison rapists unless there is overwhelming proof of guilt. The victim's word alone is rarely enough to warrant criminal prosecution. Because the victim is often a homosexual and may have been friends with the offender, the rapist's defense that he had the victim's consent is difficult to overcome. As a result, prison rapists usually suffer only prison disciplinary sanctions for their crimes.

Pending an internal investigation, both the victim and the rapist will remain in isolation. The investigation can take weeks or even months. If sufficient evidence is uncovered to support a finding that a rape occurred, then prison disciplinary proceedings will be initiated against the rapist.

Rapists are tried before a prison disciplinary hearing officer. Inevitably, the rapist will protest his innocence or claim that the incident was nothing more than a lovers' quarrel. Rapists found guilty by hearing examiners will receive several months to over a year in disciplinary custody. The length of confinement will depend on how brutal the rape was and whether there was any indication that the incident might have been consensual.

Victims who were violating prison rules when they were attacked (for example, using alcohol or drugs or being in unauthorized areas) might find themselves cited for infractions. Sometimes victims will be kept in isolation as a test of their honesty. Prison administrators believe that rape victims who are telling the truth will not protest being locked up until the incident is fully investigated. Officials consider those who complain and demand to be released from protective custody as nothing more than jilted lovers who brought false accusations against old flames to settle grudges. In any event, after reporting the rape, the victim is likely to remain in protective custody for weeks or even months.

Occasionally, either the rapist or the victim will be transferred to another prison. But more often, both will eventually be returned to the general population in the prison where the rape occurred. No matter where he ends up, the victim will have to deal with the stigma of being labeled a snitch (for reporting the rape to authorities) *and* a mark (for being raped). The victim likely will be the target of numerous other prison predators. Furthermore, the assault may become part of his "jacket" (or permanent prison record), for the world to see what another man did to him. Meanwhile, the rapist will not suffer any stigma at all, and may even enjoy an elevation in his prison status for his violent reputation.

The Tactics of Prison Rape

The victims of prison rape are almost always inmates. Cases where prisoners rape staff members are rare. Even during prison riots, guards are seldom raped; rapes that occur in riots generally involve prisoners taken from protective custody, especially snitches, debtors, and homosexuals. Furthermore, officials deal with prison rapes differently, depending on who the victims are. While the rape of an inmate is trivialized, the rape of a staff member is considered a serious felony.

Gang bangers often rely on rape in prison to generate fear and to maintain power over the general population. While street gangs use gunplay and murder to gain power, prison gangs use the threat of rape to dominate inmates and to ensure the repayment of even small debts. Some prison gangs require new inmates to commit rape as a gang initiation ritual. The act of raping another inmate is viewed as a way for gang members to demonstrate courage, strength, and cunning.

Inmate-on-Inmate Rape

Strong-Arm Rape. Strong-arm prison rape is employed by violent sexual predators. What this rapist looks for in a mark is someone who is young, attractive, frightened, physically weak, and a loner or a "fish" (a newcomer to prison). Loners and fish are good targets because they have no one who will come to their defense. Victims can be heterosexuals or homosexuals, but jailhouse virgins (who've never been sodomized) are preferred, because rapists can boast about turning them out.

Some strong-arm rapists stalk marks until they catch them in isolated parts of the prison. Others attack marks early in the morning, when most inmates' cells have been unlocked for breakfast. (This time is chosen because some inmates, especially fish, sleep through breakfast. If the rapist is lucky, the mark will be caught asleep in his cell, or at least won't be fully awake.) Strong-arm rapists generally act alone; those who attack in gangs enjoy watching victims repeatedly sodomized.

Most strong-arm rapists fear identification, so they often wear masks and/or ambush victims from behind. Some strong-arm rapists use blankets to cover victims' heads when they attack them (prisoners call this a "blanket party"). Others club their victims on the back of the head, knocking them unconscious to avoid detection.

Particularly violent strong-arm rapists keep their marks conscious during their attacks, sometimes challenging them to "fuck or fight," because they derive pleasure from overpowering struggling victims. The more the victim squirms or cries out in pain, the more enjoyment the rapist experiences; an unconscious victim provides little excitement. Some strong-arm rapists force marks to look at their attackers and to watch the attacks, boldly displaying their power over victims.

Extortion Rape. Extortion rape is very common in prisons today. It is effective because it exploits the addictions of many inmates while taking advantage of the inability of officials in overcrowded prisons to control the trade in contraband.

Extortion rape is committed by common jailhouse hustlers, such as drug dealers, bookies, and loan sharks. Potential victims are the customers of the rapist's prison hustle. Even when it isn't actually practiced, the threat of extortion rape is often used by gang members and lone prison merchants as a tool to force the repayment of debts.

The rapist learns all he needs to know about his victim during their business dealings. The ideal victim for extortion rape is a drug-addicted, physically weak inmate who is unable to pay his debts and is unaligned to any prison gang. Like strong-arm rapists, extortion rapists are equal-opportunity offenders, preying on both heterosexuals and homosexuals.

The tactic of extortion rape begins when the rapist presents himself to the eventual victim as a dealer in prison contraband. The rapist typically offers to sell the mark cigarettes, drugs, or hootch at going prison rates. If the mark doesn't have the cash to pay for these goods, the jailhouse hustler/extortion rapist will advance him credit, at an interest rate of two for one (meaning two dollars are owed for every one dollar that is advanced). The extortion rapist will continue to advance the mark credit for contraband, letting interest debts roll up rather than insisting on repayment. When the debts become too large to repay, the rapist asserts his control by physically beating the mark when his demands for repayment go unmet.

Assuming that the mark still cannot cover his debts, the extortion rapist will cunningly require him to perform some service to offset part of the loan. Should the mark refuse, he will be beaten again. The rapist usually forces the mark to work off his debt by smuggling drugs into the prison through the visiting room. This can be easily accomplished by putting one of the rapist's friends on the mark's visitation list. When this friend arrives, the mark will be given contraband, which he smuggles into prison by inserting it in his rectum. This is a crucial step for the extortion rapist: not only has he forced the mark to engage in a serious criminal act, he has compelled him to penetrate his anus with a foreign object. This brings sodomy close to the victim, although he still has no idea what is about to happen.

For a while, the rapist will use the mark as a "mule" to smuggle drugs, still selling him contraband on credit. Eventually, though, the mark will be raped as a punishment for his failure to repay debts. The extortion rapist will dismiss the seriousness of the attack, rationalizing that coerced anal sex is no worse than using one's rectum to smuggle drugs.

After the first rape, many more follow. Through a combination of physical force, shame, and addiction, the mark is transformed into a sex slave. Eventually, the extortion rapist will sell the mark's body and services to anyone willing to pay.

Because they have participated in drug smuggling, victims of extortion rape seldom report the crime to prison authorities. Snitching would land the mark in protective custody, where he couldn't satisfy his addiction to drugs or to hootch. Once they have been repeatedly violated, most victims of extortion rape would rather accept their status as prison whores than face drug withdrawal alone in an isolation unit.

Date Rape. Double-celling, dormitory housing, and inmate idleness have contributed to a surge in consensual homosexual activity in prisons today. This has brought about inmate courting rituals that can result in date rape.

Courting in prison occurs when an inmate contrives to be in the constant presence of a homosexual inmate. The two are seldom seen apart, accompanying each other to meals, yard, work, and anywhere else possible. The ultimate goal of the inmate-suitor is to become cellmates with his love interest, so they can live together as an exclusive couple.

The courting process is initiated in prison as a means to show sexual attraction. Courting also announces to the general population that a romance is brewing and that other suitors should stay clear. Courting serves to identify the couple as homosexual.

Prison date rapists take advantage of these courting rituals. Because they desire sexual gratification through the physical domination of victims, these rapists use romance as part of a trap designed to snare prey. Date rapists target physically and psychologically weak inmates who, they hope, won't report the crime. Unlike strong-arm and extortion rapists, though, date rapists only attack homosexuals. Prison date rapists are con artists who specialize in deception, not violent predators who work in the medium of brutality.

Often the date rapist begins to court his mark by lifting weights with him or by engaging in some other physically demanding sport. The date rapist does this under the guise of helping the mark to stay in shape or to ward off strong-arm rapists. During the weight-lifting sessions, the date rapist will demonstrate his physical superiority over the mark. This is a crucial part of the rapist's plan because it begins the process of establishing his physical and psychological dominance.

During the courting process, the date rapist will systematically isolate the mark from other inmates, looking for a suitable time and place to commit the rape. Afterwards, the mark is abandoned, while the rapist boasts about his conquest to the general population. This exposes the mark to even more danger and humiliation.

A deep sense of shame generally prevents the mark from reporting the crime to prison authorities. Even if the mark decides to report the rape, he seldom can counter the rapist's defense of consent.

Confidence Rape. Confidence rape in prison is similar to date rape because the rapist sets up his mark by gaining his trust. Unlike date rapists, though, confidence rapists derive perverse pleasure from turning out mostly heterosexual victims.

The confidence rapist usually picks his mark from among fish, who have little or no prior prison experience. The typical victim is a young, physically weak, frightened inmate, unaligned with gangs. The rapist first approaches his mark by pretending to offer assistance. Typically, this assistance involves warning the mark that other prison predators are planning to attack him. The rapist convinces the mark that he despises all forms of prison violence, and he offers protection out of his sense of "honor." The confidence rapist often will convince some of his friends to threaten the mark in his presence. Of course, the rapist will come to the mark's rescue, chasing away the attackers. This staged event not only establishes trust between the rapist and the mark, it also demonstrates the rapist's physical dominance over the mark.

The confidence rapist will claim that he is the only true friend that the mark has in prison. If the mark is a Christian, the rapist will pretend to be the most faithful disciple in the cellblock. (The rapist would claim to be Italian if the mark liked spaghetti.) This is all part of the plan to isolate the mark from other inmates so that he becomes completely dependent on the assistance and the friendship of the rapist. Gradually, the mark will become paranoid and reclusive, distrusting all other inmates. During this period, the rapist and the mark will constantly be in each other's company. Most other inmates will assume that the two are courting, although the mark won't know this because of his isolation.

Eventually, the rapist will get the mark to invite him into his cell or, better still, convince him that the two should double-cell together. Once they are together in a cell, it is just a matter of time until the rapist strikes. Victims of confidence rape usually are too scared to report the attack, and even if they do report it, the rapist's defense of consent will be difficult to overcome. Of course, once other inmates learn about the mark's reputation for weakness, he will be the target of other rapists.

Confidence rape is so common in prisons today that it has inspired the conventional wisdom that convicts must immediately punch strangers in the face when they offer any form of assistance or help.

Drug-Rape. This is a variation of confidence rape that involves drugs rather than fear in order to trap marks. Here, the rapist develops a tight drug relationship with the mark. The two take drugs together and usually traffic in drugs. A strong bond forms between the rapist and the victim, based on a common addiction and a shared financial interest.

Eventually, the rapist will convince the mark that the two should double-cell together to further their enterprise. One day the mark will get so high on drugs or hootch that he passes out, and the rapist then strikes. Sometimes the mark won't even realize that the rape occurred. Those who know they've been raped rarely report the crime because prison officials will claim that they sealed their own fate by dealing drugs.

Staff-on-Inmate Rape

While staff-on-inmate rape is not nearly as common as inmate-on-inmate rape, it has devastating results because of the enormous power that prison officials wield over inmates. Staff-on-inmate rape is seldom reported because victims fear retaliation, and because staff members refuse to acknowledge the incidents.

Strong-Arm Rape. Staff-on-inmate strong-arm rape occurs when a prison staff member overpowers an inmate and rapes him. Most victims of the crime are openly homosexual. This form of rape rarely occurs in the general prison population because of staff members' fear of detection. Instead, strong-arm rape occurs in disciplinary or protective custody units, where staff members can corner prisoners in complete isolation.

These assaults appear to be the result of the sexual impulses of rapists, which suggests that some prison staff members are homosexuals. The preferred victims for these assaults are inmates who have no personal or written contact with friends or family outside the prison. Because staff members have access to personal files, they can easily identify the perfect inmate-victims.

Authority-Rape. Like strong-arm rape, authority-rape occasionally occurs when homosexual staff members are physically attracted to inmates. Generally, inmate-victims are homosexuals, but this isn't always the case.

Sometimes the authority-rapist uses his power over inmate-victims to offer privileges—preferred work details or special visitation rights—in exchange for sex. At other times, rapists deny entitlements, such as positive parole reports, until victims agree to have sex. Some offer not to write-up inmates for disciplinary infractions in exchange for sex.

In these situations, it is often difficult to know for sure if staff members are taking advantage of inmate-victims or if inmates are using sex for special privileges. Regardless of the willingness of inmate-victims, any time staff members use positions of authority to grant privileges or entitlements in exchange for sex, a rape has occurred.

Surrogate Rape. Unlike staff strong-arm or authority-rapes, surrogate rapes aren't products of sexual drives. These rapes occur when prison staff members punish inmate-victims by having them "set-up" for rape by other inmates. Surrogate rapists approach a known inmate sexual predator, offering immunity from punishments and special privileges if he will rape selected inmate-victims. These rapes can occur in the general inmate population or in isolation units.

Surrogate rapes are seldom documented in prisons because of staff conspiracies of silence. The victims of surrogate rape are often inmates convicted for particularly repulsive crimes, such as child-molesters, or inmates who have filed official grievances or law suits against staff members.

A Personal Encounter

One thing that I've learned in my 17 years of incarceration is that prisoners constantly search for weaknesses that they can exploit in other inmates. Since rape is a tactic that the strong practice on the weak, it should be no surprise that some prisoners use the threat of sexual assault to test the strength of others.

Over my years of imprisonment, I've been propositioned for sex several times. Brushes with sexual assault are sometimes so subtle that fish may not immediately know that they've been sexually approached. As one prisoner put it when I interviewed him for this chapter: "Every convict's been 'cracked-on' (sexually propositioned), whether he knows it or not. And any man who says otherwise is either lying or he just don't know what time it is."

I was "cracked-on" the first day that I arrived at Holmesburg County Prison (in Philadelphia) in 1980. I was terrified as I entered Holmesburg, wearing street clothes that were drenched in perspiration. I remember that my own odor added significantly to my sense of fear.

Two guards led me into a holding room, where I encountered a powerfully built inmate who stood at least 6 feet, 5 inches, and who weighed at least 250 pounds. This man's name was Sherman, and he impatiently asked me what size clothes I wore. After I told him, he disappeared silently into a hallway.

The lone prison guard who supervised the room ordered me to strip, so when Sherman returned with my jail uniform, I was completely naked. As I quickly dressed, Sherman swaggered over to me, until he towered above me. As he glared down at me, he told me in a deep, gruff voice that jail conditions were dangerous and that if I requested to be his cellmate, he would "look out" for me.

Overcoming my fear, I forcefully refused Sherman's offer. At the time, I thought that Sherman was simply trying to bully me and extort money. It didn't occur to me until later that he was pressuring me for sex. I've since learned that many sexual approaches in prison do not involve threats or violence.

I sometimes shudder to think what may have happened to me if I had been so intimidated that I accepted Sherman's offer for protection. I was strong enough to pass this test of weakness, along with others that I've endured in prison. For inmates who fail these tests, prison becomes one long ordeal after another in a never-end-ing nightmare. Because over 90 percent of these victims will be released back into the community, the nightmare of prison rape inevitably haunts us all.

Chapter 18

Relationships Between Inmates and Guards

Editors' Note

Prisoners and their keepers have little in common. Yet as the author notes, the routine personal relationships between prisoners and guards are an important component of the larger social system within prisons. His analysis of these relationships highlights the importance of the socialization of neophyte staff.

When I first entered prison, I was surprised to discover that there was no open hostility between guards and inmates. As a matter of fact, many inmates and guards went out of their way to establish good relationships with each other. Inmates befriended guards in the hope that they would get such benefits as an extra phone call, special shower time, or the overlooking of some minor infraction. In turn, guards befriended inmates because they wanted to get information or just to keep the peace and make it through another day without getting hurt.

From what I have observed, most guards who have been attacked were attempting to enforce some petty rule. Over time, guards have learned that it doesn't always pay to be too rigid about prison regulations. Thus, an unwritten agreement has been established between inmates and guards: inmates get what they want by being friendly and nonaggressive, while guards ensure their own safety by not strictly enforcing the rules. For the most part, inmates manipulate the guards' desire for safety, and guards exploit the inmates' need for autonomy.

By the mid-1980s, things changed with overcrowding and the influx of new prison subcultures. Administrators could not hire new guards fast enough to keep pace with the flood of inmates, so the practice of overtime was employed. Any guard who was willing to work overtime could get it, with the result that on any given day a large percentage of guards were on overtime. This phenomenon had the immediate impact of introducing many exhausted, irritable guards into the work force, often on shifts with which they were not familiar.

These two factors virtually destroyed all sense of continuity and uniform treatment that the prison had established over the years. The most important element needed to maintain a workable relationship between inmates and staff is a continuity of treatment. Disturb the inmates' expectation of that continuity, and you destroy the delicate balance between them and the staff.

A tired, overworked guard on an unfamiliar shift tends to be unwilling to offer any assistance. Being a stranger to the unique inmate hierarchy of his newly assigned unit, he is unable to conform to longstanding customs and practices. This often spells disaster, as once workable relations between keeper and kept deteriorate into anger, distrust, and hatred. It has been my experience that this breakdown in relations inevitably provokes an upsurge of violence, disorder, and rioting.

There is an even more insidious consequence of excessive overtime that undermines inmate and guard relationships. In every prison there is a percentage of guards who are so rigid and unpopular with inmates, or so incompetent, that they are given work assignments that keep them away from contact with prisoners, such as tower duty or the late-night shift. Any prison administrator of intelligence knows that these kinds of guards can jeopardize the tenuous order and operation of a prison. With the advent of unlimited overtime, however, these guards have found their way into the prison mainstream. As expected, their presence has further exacerbated an already tense and uncertain environment.

The overexposure of tired, irritable, overworked, and sometimes inexperienced and antagonistic guards to the population has created an inconsistent and unpredictable prison environment, especially because guards know much less about what inmates are thinking, and vice versa. With all the new inmates coming in and out of prisons every year, it is becoming increasingly difficult for the staff to keep track of who is who and who is doing what, and even harder for a prison security force trying to employ traditional investigative and intelligence methods. In the old days, everyone knew each other in a prison and knew pretty well what everyone else was up to. Not so today.

The only way the security system can effectively operate in a prison today is by soliciting the services of snitches. Guards maintain a legion of snitches and openly advertise that fact to the inmate population. In order to keep their informants in force, prison administrators have gone overboard to reward and protect them. Their rationale is that every informant constitutes an unpaid member of the security force that helps to compensate for understaffing. This almost exclusive reliance on informants for information and intelligence creates several conditions, including:

1. Keeping the inmate population at odds with each other over who is the informant in their midst.

2. Elevating snitches in the prison hierarchy, since they are often rewarded with the best jobs, highest pay, and best living conditions.

3. Increasing the growing antagonism between long-term inmates and parole violators, who are more likely to become informants in order to gain early parole and relative comfort during their brief stay in prison.

4. A proliferation of drugs entering the prison, as informants act as conduits for drug smuggling while looking for information.

5. Providing prison administrators with distorted images of inmate activity, as informants become less credible the more they are used.

This last condition often occurs because an informant is pursuing his own interests and therefore will only inform on those activities that do not affect his particular business. Such self-serving information is only as accurate as the informant needs it to be. Some-times it is a fabricated reflection of what he knows the administration wants to hear. Thus, many informants provide the kind of information that sacrifices the truth in order to conform to some pre-existing view.

To use a classic example of this, I knew an ambitious guard in 1983 who told me he used his overtime to ensure himself a more substantial pension benefit. (In those days, pensions were based on the three highest annual salaries rather than on base salary.) So he worked double shifts seven days a week for three years. But as a result, he became useless. He was either too listless and irritable or falling asleep all the time. In order to convince his superiors of his efficiency, he would reward informants who gave him information that he could use to issue misconducts. Consequently, his informants were in turn able to operate a massive drug and homosexual prostitu-tion ring under his protection. Administrators ended up buying a nickel's worth of information for $1,000's worth of corruption.

Another example involved a prison murder. One day in the yard, two inmates fought over drugs until one of them was stabbed to death in plain view of dozens of witnesses. Subsequently, the prison security officer received numerous notes from inmates wish-ing to give eyewitness accounts. This enabled the authorities to quickly identify the culprit. But the informants all gave self-serving details of the crime and its motives, until there were so many con-tradicting versions of what happened that all their testimony was rendered worthless. Without enough evidence, the state was forced to offer the murderer five to ten years in return for a guilty plea. Such a sentence for a murder committed in a public prison yard is so lenient that it could be considered a license to kill. This failure of justice on the part of the prison administration was precipitated by its exclusive reliance on unreliable informants.

The end result is that today's prisons have become even more violent. Inmates do not trust each other, because informants call the shots and even initiate or encourage most of the crimes they report. Guards are overworked and increasingly alienated from the main-stream of prison life. And finally, a new breed of criminals—young, violent, ignorant, drug-addicted, and completely self-absorbed—is pouring in and leaving even the most veteran inmates and staff scared to death.

Chapter 19

A Theory of Prison Evolution

Editors' Note

The author's view of prison adaptation, or evolution, attributes the recent breakdown of American prisons to overcrowding. In simplest terms, each prison has a natural population capacity, based on its design, infrastructure, and resources. When the prison's natural capacity is exceeded, it is launched into an unpredictable trajectory. Hassine illustrates this theory with the example of Graterford.

At a recent group-counseling session I heard someone say that the problem with prisons today is that they no longer have any direction. That statement hit me like a lock in a sock, as I came to a realization: Graterford had no direction, so the gangs, thieves, extortionists, and the walls themselves provided direction in the only way they could—through greed and brutality.

In the early and mid-1980s, Graterford was a prison that maintained control by establishing *no* controls. The only rule that was strictly applied was "Don't try to escape," and the walls made this easy to enforce. Everything else was up for grabs. Ironically, this anarchic style of prison management was fairly effective. Inmates spent so much time protecting themselves from each other that few had the opportunity to even consider escape. Additionally, the high rate of inmate murders and death by drug overdose ultimately maintained the prison society's own form of population control.

If there is any lesson to be learned from Graterford, it is in the *evolution* of prisons: how factors in a prison's design, management, structure, and inmate population can work with and against each other in its transition from a prison to a tribe of gangs to a kingdom of inmates.

To better understand some of the underlying factors, we should consider the original design concept of Graterford itself. It would be safe to say that the prison's builders followed the principle that a larger prison is a better prison; hence its five mammoth cell blocks and its gigantic walls. But an unforeseen factor ultimately crippled this bigger-is-better theory of prison design: the huge cost it would take to supervise the 2,144 inmates Graterford was originally intended to hold. With the advent of the Great Depression and World War II, spending a fortune to maintain an oversized prison colony grew less and less practical.

For four decades, the inmate population at Graterford remained manageably small and well below capacity, so the prison's design had yet to be tested. Its only serious drawbacks at the time were the obvious conditions of too little manpower to supervise too many inmates and the extraordinary length of the blocks that made visual observation difficult. The inmate population surge of the 1970s changed all that, causing the inherent failure of Graterford's design to become alarmingly apparent: bigger was *not* better.

It is my contention that the growth of a prison population beyond 1,500 inmates is most likely to trigger a prison's process of degenerative evolution. That threshold figure can be much lower if the prison is grossly understaffed and/or mismanaged. Generally, the faster an inmate population grows beyond 1,500, the more unpredictable that population becomes.

The struggle for control over a prison can be likened to a game of chess: whoever maintains control of the center of the board is likely to dominate the whole board and win the game. If the center in this analogy is the greater mass of an inmate population, then an administration must control its movement and conduct in order to maintain control of the prison. The biggest concerns for management are the fringes of the population outside the center: convicts who are unresponsive to any form of control or imposed discipline, including prison gang leaders, rapists, rabble-rousers, sociopaths, and prison assassins.

The chief factor for control of a prison's center is the protection of the inmate population. Inmates in general will follow the path perceived to be the safest. To control the center, the administration has to keep the fringes from creating so much fear and disorder that inmates move outside the center to find safety, which can happen spontaneously and unpredictably.

As the inmate center grows in size, so too does the inmate fringe. Once the number of inmates outside the center becomes so great that groups and sub-groups begin to form, their ability to adversely influence conditions in the center will increase dramatically. Consequently, the administration will need more manpower and financial resources to maintain a safe and orderly environment at the center. Even with sufficient funds and staffing, a prison administration will be hard pressed to overcome the destabilizing effects of such powerful fringe elements as they consolidate their forces. If management cannot meet all the needs of the expanding inmate center, then its control of that center becomes weaker, while the destructive power of the inmate fringe grows stronger.

If the general population grows so rapidly that the prison staff can no longer protect those in the center, small, secure groups will form until the whole prison population becomes a collection of fringe groups seeking protection. The administration's control will then be limited to only basic physical confinement.

At this point, the prison has evolved into a collective tribe made up of clans working independently of and at odds with each other. Now anything can happen, as the fringe groups further explore the limits of their power and the prison administration responds with more desperate measures to regain control. While the staff may still control some parts of the center, its authority is so undermined that it is treated as just another clan.

During this tribal stage, the inmate population becomes extremely sensitive to changes in its composition. For example, as more violent or drug-addicted inmates enter the system, their potential to destabilize the prison skyrockets as the weakened prison administration's ability to neutralize them plummets.

Once the mounting chaos within the prison population begins to crystallize into a common identity and self-awareness on the part of the inmates, the prison will evolve into a kingdom. Clans will work together to ensure that the administration can never reestablish control of the center. While these clans will continue to challenge each other for dominance, no one clan can ever muster enough resources to maintain total control.

Graterford serves as a fitting example of an evolving prison. During the 1970s, its inmate population increased so rapidly in inverse proportion to decreasing staff and funding that its evolution was inevitable. At that time, a growing number of gang members flooded into Graterford as the result of a surge of gang wars in Philadelphia. In 1969, Eastern Penitentiary was shut down and a large number of inner-city African-American inmates wound up in Graterford. These conditions only served to accelerate Graterford's entry into the tribal stage.

When I arrived at Graterford in 1981, the population was at an all-time high of 1,800 and the administration had already lost control over its epidemic of violence. As described earlier by Double D, it apparently made one last attempt to establish control of the center by empowering Rocky and his gang to neutralize the activities of the fringe. But when the clans united to run Rocky out of the prison, the administration not only lost more control, but the Kingdom of Inmates learned the effectiveness of organization.

Chicken Sunday marked the final stage of Graterford's evolution into a kingdom, when inmates realized for the first time that *they*, and not the staff, controlled the space within its concrete walls. Hence, they joined forces to protect their interests against the administration's and defend the underground economy.

As I look back on the failure of Graterford as a system of social engineering, I remember how quickly guards and inmates alike retrogressed from order to anarchy. I realize now that the consequences of such a failed social system *outside* these walls could be even more terrifying. Civilization can be as fragile as our freedom, and the same men who today stand for all that is good in the world can tomorrow turn into savage barbarians who exploit the weak.

Graterford remains to this day a harsh reminder of how a dense concentration of men left to fend for themselves can create a Darwinian tidal pool of lifeforms perfected by hardships—an evolutionary process that ensures the survival of only the strongest and the most resourceful.

Chapter 20

Conclusion: The Runaway Train

Editors' Note

The author's analogy here suggests that the problems facing American prisons will inevitably lead to cataclysm. Impending doom has been a constant theme of American prisons and prison reform movements. For nearly three centuries, American prisons have confronted one crisis after another and, surviving each one, have gone on relatively unchanged. To be sure, many of the system components that we take for granted today—for example, probation and parole—are products of these crises. The author believes that the challenges facing American prisons today may be more cataclysmic than any past crisis.

Overcrowding is the harbinger of cataclysmic change in our nation's prison system. That change is so profound that it is transforming the very structure and operation of the entire system, not just individual prisons. On the one hand, it is giving birth to a renegade bureaucracy obsessed with maintaining its own uncertain existence in the struggle to retain control over the penal system. On the other hand, it is creating a terrified population of inmates who have lost all sense of security and live like "moment dwellers" with no thought of the future.

To better understand the nature and extent of this transformation, consider the analogy of a runaway train. Imagine you're a passenger on a train. As you travel along, you sense that your train is moving faster than usual. This does not alarm you, but you stop reading your newspaper, take a look at your watch, then peer out a window. You notice the countryside whizzing past you at an increasing rate. Suddenly you see the train speed past the station where you were supposed to get off.

Now you are alarmed. But a voice over the loudspeaker apologizes for the inconvenience, assures everyone that everything is under control, and promises the train will stop at the next station. The train continues to accelerate.

Soon, the train hurtles past yet another station. You begin to realize that something is seriously wrong. You try to find a conductor or anyone in authority, but you get caught in a crush of passengers who have decided to do the same thing. Again you hear the loudspeaker voice, but because of all the confusion you can't make out what it is saying. In any event, you no longer trust any announcements. The train plunges forward out of control, faster and faster.

The crowd, the uncertainty, and the noise cause panic. It is at this point that the train has been transformed from a vehicle of mass transit to a machine that spreads pandemonium among passengers, who now face an uncertain future.

As panic and confusion rise, desperation sets in. No one cares anymore about their jobs, their schedules, or their futures. Everyone is thinking about right now and how they are going to survive this madness. Every human intuition has surrendered to the primitive instincts of "survival of the fittest." The passengers are no longer passengers, and the train is no longer a train.

Now imagine that you are the train engineer. You were the first to realize the train's acceleration problem. Because you are a trained expert, you felt certain you would be able to fix any mechanical problem. You radio the next station and inform them of the problem, then you pull out your repair manual and go about trying to fix the engine. But the train continues to accelerate and refuses to respond to any of your efforts. At this point you begin to worry.

As you work feverishly to control the train, you hear passengers banging on your engineer's door. The frustration of your failed efforts, the loud din of the uncooperative engine, and the panicking cries of passengers combine to unnerve you. You angrily take a moment to bark over the loudspeaker, "Everything is under control—please remain in your seats." But the screams and banging intensify as the train continues to accelerate beyond your control. You need help but you know you're not going to get any.

Despite your desperate and futile efforts, you realize that the longer you fail to slow your train, the more problems you'll be forced to fix. Weaknesses in design and construction of the train have caused additional mechanical failures. You find yourself reacting to a multitude of new emergencies that give you little or no opportunity to address the original problem. You know that unless this acceleration is stopped, collision or derailment is imminent.

At this point, you are no longer a trained professional concerned only with train schedules and engine maintenance. You have become a reactionary crisis-control manager who no longer cares where the train is headed. Your main goal now is to avert a catastrophe, and you have to keep those hysterical passengers from interfering with what you're trying to do. Meanwhile, the train races faster and faster.

Now imagine that you are a commuter on a train station platform. All of a sudden you see a train speed past you. You catch a glimpse of passengers banging on the passing windows. You notice that their faces show hysteria and that some of them are holding up signs, which you can't make out because the train is out of control, a runaway.

What you have seen causes you some fear and anxiety until you hear an authoritative voice over a loudspeaker apologizing for the inconvenience and announcing that everything is well under control. You are instructed to wait calmly until your train arrives. Though a bit perplexed, you are at least relieved that *you* will be able to reach your destination on time and in one piece.

The message of this parable is clear. I am one of those hysterical passengers on the runaway train, and this book is a sign that I'm waving at my window, hoping against hope that someone outside the train can read it and get help to us before a catastrophe destroys us all. Prison administrators are the frantic engineers trying to keep me and the other hysterical passengers out of their way while they work to bring the runaway train back under control.

And you, my readers, are the people calmly standing in the station as we tear by. You live in a normal world with all of its normal worries, such as whether your train will be on time or whether you will be late for work. A brief glimpse of our frantic faces may disturb your normal world for a moment.

Will you assume that everything is really all right and go back to reading your newspapers? Or will you to try to get help to those passengers who, in the final analysis, are fellow human beings on the train of life?

Afterword

Richard A. Wright
Arkansas State University

Throughout the history of incarceration, countless prisoners have written books about their experiences behind bars. "Prose and cons" appear to go together like love and marriage, as articulate, curious inmates find the right mixture of spare time, exotic subject matter, and memorable characters to fill their notebooks. This is why writing courses and inmate newspapers and newsletters thrive in most prisons.

It should be no surprise, then, that penitentiaries have transformed aspiring writers into skilled essayists (see Abbott 1982; Jackson 1970) or even brilliant authors (see Genet [1949] 1964; Solzhenitsyn 1974, 1975, 1976). As a criminologist whose specialty is corrections, I have read numerous books written by prisoners. None offers more insight into the daily routines and everyday crises in contemporary American prisons than Victor Hassine's *Life Without Parole*.

For me, this book is like spending a few days wandering through the cellblocks of a men's maximum-security prison. Those familiar with these institutions will find the characters and situations described by Hassine credible and vivid. For students and lay persons, no rival work offers a superior, word-for-word introduction to modern prison life.

What follows are some reflections about how Hassine's book relates to certain larger issues in social research and the correctional literature, concluding with a few thoughts about the policy implications of *Life Without Parole*.

Victor Hassine, Graterford, and External Validity

Social scientists are always concerned about whether their observations are idiosyncratic or can be generalized to other persons, settings, and situations. This is because researchers usually only have sufficient resources to survey a handful among the throng of individuals who share the particular characteristics they are interested in studying. In scientific jargon, this problem is known as *external validity*: Is one's sample representative of some larger population (see Babbie 1992; Denzin 1989)?

External validity is a particularly serious problem in life-histories research, where one individual in one setting tries to speak for many persons in different places (Denzin 1989). Although a number of famous studies in criminology are life-histories of one offender (e.g., Shaw 1930; Sutherland 1937) or small groups of offenders (e.g., Ianni 1972; Whyte 1943), some scholars dismiss most examples of these works as biased.

On the surface of things, the demand for external validity would seem to pose insurmountable problems of interpretation in the cases of Victor Hassine and Graterford. Hassine himself remarks that when he first arrived at Graterford he was a "square john," prison slang for a middle-class, law-abiding inmate who usually identifies more with the staff than with other inmates. Few square johns end up in maximum-security prisons, but most who do are murderers. The square-john killer is a rare breed in maximum security, sharing nothing more than an address with the lower-class career criminals confined to the rest of the cellblock. Even more unusual, Hassine is a Jewish immigrant from Egypt who holds a law degree. This combination of factors makes him a truly unique prisoner.

Although the State Correctional Institution at Graterford is certainly more representative of American prisons than Victor Hassine is of American prisoners, there are still problems in generalizing from Graterford to other correctional settings. Graterford, which I have visited along with many other correctional institutions throughout the United States, is an infamous men's "big house" penitentiary—the last stop for Pennsylvania's most dangerous male felons. There are no other prisons like it in the state; for similarities, one must consider such notorious institutions as Stateville Penitentiary in Illinois, Kansas State Penitentiary in Lansing, Huntsville Prison in Texas, Washington State Penitentiary in Walla Walla, or the federal penitentiaries in Marion, Illinois and Leavenworth, Kansas. Gangs, drugs, violence, and corruption are much more common in these penitentiaries than in other types of prisons that have fewer menacing inmates and custody complications.

In Graterford, Victor Hassine was a unique prisoner confined in an unusual setting. Normally, this combination would create an external validity nightmare. In *Life Without Parole*, however, Hassine writes more about fellow inmates in ordinary prison situations than about his own experiences at Graterford. This strategy converts a potential methodological catastrophe into a genuine success.

While Hassine and Graterford may be atypical, those familiar with prisons will immediately recognize the other types on his cellblock: the contorted face and broken gait of Chaser, strung out on psychotropics; the slumping, defeated Albert Brown as he shuffles outside his deserted cell; the scheming, manipulative Clarence, plotting to trick the Program Review Committee; the drunken, bellowing Hammerhead, guzzling hootch as he runs from the hacks. The situations described by Hassine are everyday occurrences in many prisons: the swag men brazenly hawking sandwiches to their customers; the gruesome tasks of the "meat wagon crews" loading victims of drug overdoses and violence onto their gurneys; "the inmate's dilemma" of what to do when confronting a burglar caught ransacking one's cell; the punk's dilemma of whether to "fuck or fight" a hulking "strong-arm" rapist.

Hassine overcomes part of the problem of external validity by giving the reader a panoramic view of modern prison life rather than a retrospective self-portrait. *Life Without Parole* captures the atmosphere of crushing boredom, endless routine, mindless amusement, and occasional gripping fear that almost every inmate experiences every moment in every American prison.

Deprivation or Importation?

Correctional researchers have long recognized that a distinctive inmate subculture—with separate norms, values, attitudes, beliefs, and language—flourishes in prison (see Carroll [1974] 1988, 1977; Clemmer 1940; Goffman 1961; Irwin [1970] 1987; Irwin and Cressey 1962; Jacobs 1977; Sykes 1958). Strong evidence of this prisoner subculture is found in Chapter 1 ("How I Became a Convict"), especially when Hassine notes how jailhouse slang unifies inmates into "one big clan," and in Chapter 5 ("The Underground Economy"), where he comments on the "Inmate Code of Conduct" in Graterford.

There is a heated debate among scholars about the origins of this subculture. Those supporting the "deprivation model" argue that the "pains of imprisonment"—including the losses of liberty, material goods and services, heterosexual relationships, autonomy, and personal security—contribute to the formation of a peculiar inmate society with well-defined prisoner roles (see Clemmer 1940; Goffman 1961; in particular Sykes 1958). Hassine recalls that he received his first misconduct charge in Graterford because he missed "one of life's simplest pleasures: a fresh cooked hamburger." He purchased ten pounds of frozen ground beef from a swag man, a convict who specializes in providing goods and services to prisoners who desire the material comforts of the outside world. Deprivation theorists argue that complex inmate societies, of which swag men are only a small part, have an "indigenous origin" (Sykes 1958): the hardships of confinement lead to the development of a criminogenic subculture found only within prisons.

Proponents of the "importation model" counter that the inmate subculture is not a response to the isolation and deprivations of imprisonment, but instead is brought into the prison from the streets (see Carroll [1974] 1988, 1977; Jacobs 1977; in particular Irwin [1970] 1987; Irwin and Cressey 1962). The importation model views pre-prison experiences as the most important factors shaping the development of prison subcultures. For example, Irwin and Cressey (1962) argue that prison subcultures and prisoner roles for the most part are not adjustments to the deprivations of confinement; rather they are composites of various criminal and conventional street identities that are imported into the prison. As one example, Hassine is a square john to the other convicts because of the law-abiding, middle-class values and conventional identity he carried with him from the outside world.

The consensus among most correctional scholars is that the importation model is the superior explanation for the inmate subcultures found in modern American prisons (Wright 1994; for a different view, see Hunt, Riegal, Morales, and Waldorf 1993). In the 1960s and early 1970s, correctional reforms and federal court decisions eased some of the pains of imprisonment, making it easier for prisoners to retain their street identities and lifestyles (Carroll [1974] 1988, 1977; Jacobs 1977). Among the correctional reforms, Carroll and Jacobs note that the liberalization of visitation, telephone, and mail privileges, and the permission to wear street clothes and hairstyles, to decorate their cells, and to bring television sets and radios into prisons enabled inmates to maintain close contact with the outside world and to preserve their pre-prison, street personalities. United States Supreme Court decisions extended the freedom of religion to prisoners (in *Cooper v. Pate*, 1964), virtually abolished the censoring of inmate mail by prison officials (in *Procunier v. Martinez*, 1974), and extended limited constitutional protections to inmates (in *Wolff v. McDonnell*, 1974), further reducing the isolation of prisoners from society.

Although Hassine describes the deprivations of imprisonment—including the losses of heterosexual love, possessions, privacy, peace and quiet, and personal security—*Life Without Parole* offers stronger support for the importation model. Hassine observes that in the early 1980s the "ghetto evils of the decaying American inner city" were compressed into Graterford. He notes that almost overnight gang bangers, drug addicts and dealers, the homeless, the mentally ill, and juvenile offenders poured into the penitentiary, disrupting prison life and routines. The violent, addictive, acquisitive, disorganized lifestyles of the new inmates (now called "the Pepsi Generation" in current prison slang; Fong, Vogel, and Buentello 1996; Hunt et al. 1993) especially offended the Old Heads, who longed for the good old days when the *"outside world was kept outside."*

Hassine's comments in Chapter 7 ("Race Relations in Prison") about prison gangs bolster the importation position. (For a sociological analysis of the effect of street gangs in Stateville Penitentiary, see Jacobs 1977.) Although some gangs apparently have had an indigenous origin in other prisons (see Hunt et al. 1993), Hassine claims that at Graterford, inmate organizations among both African Americans and whites are dominated by gangs that once roamed the streets. Philadelphia neighborhood gangs bearing specific street names—e.g., the 10th Street Gang—govern interactions among African Americans; outlaw motorcycle gangs from rural Pennsylvania organize white prisoners. These prison gangs imported their roles, organizational structures, and leadership styles directly from the

streets. Prison gang members often rely on their contacts with associates on the street to smuggle drugs and other contraband into
institutions (Fong, Vogel, and Buentello 1992).

Correctional practitioners and researchers now recognize that
the imposing prison walls that surround institutions like Graterford
are surprisingly permeable. While prison walls, fences, and towers
still prevent the inside world from getting outside, they can no
longer prevent the outside world—with its diverse attractions, di-
versions, and problems—from getting inside.

The Penal Harm Movement

Although correctional reforms and court decisions dramatically
lessened the deprivations experienced by prisoners in the 1960s and
early 1970s, the pains of imprisonment have since worsened. Some
scholars claim that conservative politicians are spearheading a "penal harm movement" in America today, with the intention of increasing the misery associated with punishment (Clear 1994; Cullen
1995; Simon 1993; Tonry 1995). While Cullen reminds us that corrections has always been a "mean-spirited enterprise," he contends
that the recent popularity of "three-strikes-and-you're-out" laws
(that mandate life sentences for third-felony convictions) and the
reappearance of chain gangs in Alabama are "symbolic" indicators
of the rise of penal harm. More substantively, Clear (1994, p. 50)
documents that since 1972 "every state altered its penal policy in
the direction of greater punitive severity" through such measures
as the restriction or abolition of parole release and/or the implementation of mandatory sentencing laws.

Because the penal harm movement specifically targets predatory street crime and the crack cocaine epidemic, massive numbers
of minority-group, drug-addicted, urban-underclass offenders
have entered Graterford and other American prisons during the last
decade. (For academic accounts of these developments, see Clear
1994; Simon 1993; Tonry 1995.) For prison administrators, this
means coping with overcrowding while also stretching institutional
programs and services beyond their limits to meet the extensive
needs of a diseased, drug-addicted, and illiterate inmate population. Prison officials often must meet these new demands under the
pressure of budget freezes imposed by state legislatures.

Life Without Parole superbly details the practical effect of the penal harm movement on the lives of inmates (see in particular Chapter 4, "Prison Violence"). By the mid-1980s, prison officials had apparently lost control of Graterford to rival inmate gangs; cell-blocks were filled with drugs, violence, and corruption. While assigned to the meat wagon crew, Hassine served as a medic on the frontline of penal harm. Although he argues (in Chapter 5, "The Underground Economy") that the confrontation between Double D and Rocky replaced disorganized, "tribal" gang violence with a united "Kingdom of Inmates," recent events (see Appendix A, "A State Tries to Rein in a Prison Awash in Drugs") suggest that this period of relative tranquility in Graterford was shortlived.

Through its impact on prison overcrowding (see Clear 1994), the penal harm movement has increased the deprivation suffered by virtually every inmate in America. In Chapter 16 ("Prison Over-crowding"), Hassine offers a personal account of the suffering he has experienced from double-celling. Some prisons are now triple- and even quadruple-celling inmates or requiring prisoners to sleep barracks-style in warehouses, gymnasiums, or auditoriums. Hassine argues in Chapter 17 ("Prison Rape") that these conditions have contributed to an increase in the frequency of prison rape.

In an attempt some years ago to articulate a "new ideology" for punishment, the eminent correctional scholar John Irwin sensibly argued:

> Those convicted of serious crimes must be punished and impris-oned—knowing that imprisonment itself is very punitive, we need not punish above and beyond imprisonment. This means that we need not and must not degrade, provoke, nor excessively deprive the human beings we have placed in prison.
> (1980, p. 248)

By promoting prison overcrowding, and related evils like prison rape, the penal harm movement has clearly extended degradation, provocation, and deprivation well beyond the act of imprisonment to the daily *conditions* of confinement.

The Penology of Desperation

Criminal justice theorists and philosophers of punishment end-lessly debate the appropriate rationales for criminal justice process-ing. For example, in a famous conceptualization of criminal procedure, Packer (1968) distinguishes between the crime control and the due process models. The crime control model emphasizes the efficiency of convictions, the presumption of guilt, and the va-lidity of the coercive power of the state over the offender; due process emphasizes the reliability of convictions, the presumption of innocence, and the strict protection of individual rights through the limitation of state power. Philosophers of punishment argue *ad nauseam* about the relative merits of retribution (matching the se-verity of punishments to the seriousness of crimes), rehabilitation (implementing treatment strategies and programs to reform indi-vidual offenders and to prevent future crimes), deterrence (using threatened or actual punishments to convince persons not to com-mit future crimes), and incapacitation (preventing crime in the larger society through the use of punishment to remove criminals from circulation in free society) as the rationales for correctional policies and programs.

Some recent commentators claim that these older models and rationales have little relevance to the current operations of prisons. Rutherford (1993) contends that a bureaucratic "expediency model"—that emphasizes smooth management and pragmatic ef-ficiency through adopting a procedure-based, mechanistic, emo-tionally detached administrative style—guides correctional thinking today. Feeley and Simon (1992) refer to this administrative approach as the "new penology." These authors argue that the ex-pediency model contained in the new penology is a practical re-sponse to the immediate pressures of overcrowding, violence, and disorganization in prisons.

Hassine's runaway train analogy (Chapter 20, "Conclusion") offers a far more disturbing image of current correctional opera-tions. He believes that the problems in modern prisons have become so grave that prison administrators are simply "crisis-control man-agers" whose primary goal is to "avert a catastrophe" in a "renegade bureaucracy." Overcrowded cellblocks ruled by gangs and filled with drugs and violence mean that prisoners and staff alike are only concerned about "how they are going to survive this madness." The implication is that in the last few years, correctional policy has rapidly shifted from some variation of crime control, due process, retribution, rehabilitation, deterrence, and incapacitation, through expediency, to mere survival.

Sadly, I believe that Hassine's observations are correct. It appears that some prisons in the United States are in such a condition of turmoil that many correctional officials are now more concerned about serving their tours of duty with their minds and bodies intact than seriously considering any abstract models or rationales of punishment. Because new disasters and outrages occur almost every day, prison officials must constantly improvise and adjust their actions to suit each new crisis. There is no game plan, no blueprint, and certainly no hope in all of this. After all, expediency is still a model, but survival is only an instinct.

The penal harm movement embraced by the public and politicians in the outside world has led to a "penology of desperation" on the inside. It is of urgent importance that Americans reconsider the policies that have increased the harms inflicted on prisoners, if not for captives like Victor Hassine, then at least for their captors.

References

Abbott, Jack Henry. 1982. *In the Belly of the Beast: Letters from Prison*. New York: Vintage.

Babbie, Earl. 1992. *The Practice of Social Research*. 6th ed. Belmont, CA: Wadsworth.

Carroll, Leo. (1974) 1988. *Hacks, Blacks, and Cons: Race Relations in a Maximum Security Prison*. Prospect Heights, IL: Waveland.

———. 1977. "Race and Three Forms of Prisoner Power: Confrontation, Censoriousness, and the Corruption of Authority." Pp. 40-53 in *Contemporary Corrections: Social Control and Conflict*, edited by C. Ronald Huff. Beverly Hills, CA: Sage.

Clear, Todd R. 1994. *Harm in American Penology: Offenders, Victims, and Their Communities*. Albany, NY: State University of New York Press.

Clemmer, Donald. 1940. *The Prison Community*. New York: Holt, Rinehart and Winston.

Cullen, Francis T. 1995. "Assessing the Penal Harm Movement." *Journal of Research in Crime and Delinquency* 32: 338-58.

Denzin, Norman K. 1989. *The Research Act*. 3rd ed. Englewood Cliffs, NJ: Prentice-Hall.

Feeley, Malcolm M., and Jonathan Simon. 1992. "The New Penology: Notes on the Emerging Strategy of Corrections and Its Implications." *Criminology* 30: 449-74.

Fong, Robert S., Ronald E. Vogel, and Salvador Buentello. 1992. "Prison Gang Dynamics: A Look Inside the Texas Department of Corrections." Pp. 57-77 in *Corrections: Dilemmas and Directions*, edited by Peter J. Benekos and Alida V. Merlo. Cincinnati: Anderson.

——. 1996. "Prison Gang Dynamics: A Research Update." Pp. 105-28 in *Gangs: A Criminal Justice Approach*, edited by J. Mitchell Miller and Jeffrey P. Rush. Cincinnati: Anderson.

Genet, Jean. (1949) 1964. *The Thief's Journal*. New York: Grove.

Goffman, Erving. 1961. *Asylums: Essays on the Social Situation of Mental Patients and Other Inmates*. Garden City, NY: Anchor.

Hunt, Geoffrey, Stephanie Riegal, Tomas Morales, and Dan Waldorf. 1993. "Changes in Prison Culture: Prison Gangs and the Case of the Pepsi Generation." *Social Problems* 40: 398-410.

Ianni, Francis A. J. 1972. *A Family Business: Kinship and Social Control in Organized Crime*. New York: Russell Sage Foundation.

Irwin, John. (1970) 1987. *The Felon*. Berkeley: University of California Press.

——. 1980. *Prisons in Turmoil*. Boston: Little, Brown.

Irwin, John, and Donald R. Cressey. 1962. "Thieves, Convicts, and the Inmate Culture." *Social Problems* 10: 142-55.

Jackson, George. 1970. *Soledad Brother*. New York: Bantam.

Jacobs, James B. 1977. *Stateville: The Penitentiary in Mass Society*. Chicago: University of Chicago Press.

Packer, Herbert L. 1968. *The Limits of the Criminal Sanction*. Stanford, CA: Stanford University Press.

Rutherford, Andrew. 1993. *Criminal Justice and the Pursuit of Decency*. Oxford, England: Oxford University Press.

Shaw, Clifford R. 1930. *The Jack-Roller: A Delinquent Boy's Own Story*. Chicago: University of Chicago Press.

Simon, Jonathan. 1993. *Poor Discipline: Parole and the Social Control of the Underclass, 1890-1990*. Chicago: University of Chicago Press.

Solzhenitsyn, Aleksandr I. 1974. *The Gulag Archipelago*. New York: Harper and Row.

——. 1975. *The Gulag Archipelago, Two*. New York: Harper and Row.

——. 1976. *The Gulag Archipelago, Three*. New York: Harper and Row.

Sutherland, Edwin H. 1937. *The Professional Thief*. Chicago: University of Chicago Press.

Sykes, Gresham M. 1958. *The Society of Captives: A Study of a Maximum Security Prison*. Princeton, NJ: Princeton University Press.

Tonry, Michael. 1995. *Malign Neglect: Race, Crime, and Punishment in America*. New York: Oxford University Press.

Whyte, William Foote. 1943. *Streetcorner Society*. Chicago: University of Chicago Press.

Wright, Richard A. 1994. *In Defense of Prisons*. Westport, CT: Greenwood.

Cases

Cooper v. Pate 378 U.S. 546 (1964).

Procunier v. Martinez 416 U.S. 396 (1974).

Wolff v. McDonnell 418 U.S. 539 (1974).

Appendices

Appendix A

Editors' Note

During the editing of the first edition of this book, the State Correctional Institution at Graterford experienced a system-wide breakdown, a derailment. Hundreds of corrections officers and specialists who had never before been inside Graterford were brought in to help fix the problem. What these outsiders discovered when they explored Graterford for the first time was the "Kingdom of Inmates" which Victor Hassine accurately described in this book—and which they subsequently reported on in The New York Times *article reprinted below.*

A State Tries to Rein in a Prison Awash in Drugs

Reprinted from *The New York Times,* October 30, 1995
Matthew Purdy

GRATERFORD, Pa., October 26—In February, the Pennsylvania authorities paroled Robert Simon, despite his being a convicted killer and known prison drug user who had killed another inmate in self-defense.

Three months later, back on the street, Mr. Simon was accused of another killing, this time the shooting of a New Jersey police officer who had stopped him and a fellow motorcycle gang member in Gloucester County for a traffic violation.

When the authorities in Pennsylvania began looking into why Mr. Simon was set free, the trail led back to the state prison here, where officials say the case is another sign of the widespread drug trade, mismanagement, and possible corruption at the crowded maximum-security prison outside of Philadelphia.

In the view of state corrections officials, it was as if the prison had fallen into enemy hands. Last Monday, 650 state troopers and corrections officers from other prisons

173

were deployed in a nighttime surprise assault on Graterford. During the next 72 hours, they searched all 3,500* inmates, the prison's staff, and its 1,700-acre grounds, looking for drugs and weapons. As a result, nine ranking officers at the prison retired or were transferred, and 21 inmates suspected of drug trafficking were moved to other prisons.

The shakedown, in which about 200 homemade weapons and more than 60 caches of drugs were seized, was unusual in scope. But the extreme action was an indication of the frustration many corrections officials and politicians feel at the constant battle to keep drugs out of prisons, especially as tougher laws are sending drug-addicted criminals away for longer sentences.

The question that prompted the raid—"Who runs the prison?" in the words of Martin F. Horn, Pennsylvania's Corrections Commissioner—is a common one for prison administrators. Corrections officials across the country say controlling prisons is becoming more difficult because of increasing inmate populations, harder-core prisoners, and tighter budgets. Earlier this month, inmates were ordered confined to their cells at federal prisons after uprisings at five sites.

The drug economy in prisons not only threatens peace among inmates but also dangles temptation before guards. In the last year at the federal prison in Atlanta, for example, several employees have been arrested on drug charges and there has been a spate of violence, including the first killing of a corrections officer at the prison since 1987.

(On Friday, federal prosecutors announced the indictments of four corrections officers, four inmates, and two others on charges of trying to smuggle marijuana, cocaine, and heroin into the Atlanta prison.)

"In large systems, it's almost a truism that you're going to have some drug trafficking," said a former Texas prison official and a consultant on prison conditions, Steve Martin. "But when it seeps into your security staff you have serious problems."

Governor Tom Ridge of Pennsylvania, who approved the search of Graterford, said, "The first thing we need to do is control the prisons, and we weren't in control of that one."

Officials said that in Mr. Simon's case a complete record of his prison misdeeds was not in his file when the parole decision was made. Inmates told a recent State Senate hearing that it was common practice among prisoners at Graterford to avoid punishment for infractions and to cover up evidence of drug use by paying officers to alter records.

At the hearing, an inmate who was a clerk at Graterford from 1992 to this January, Jonathan Brown, told the State Senate Judiciary Committee about officers' selling furloughs and other privileges, and about drug trafficking among officers. He said Mr. Simon paid officers to cover up his disciplinary infractions, though the allegations have not been proved and are under investigation.

"The fact that he was allegedly selling and using dope was not in his file," said the committee chairman, Senator Stewart J. Greenleaf.

Mr. Simon's case was just more evidence of trouble at Graterford, one of the largest state prisons in the country. Since 1989, 13 staff members have been arrested on charges of trying to smuggle drugs, 11 inmates have died of drug overdoses, and about 20 percent of the urine tests done on prisoners each month show signs of drug use.

In March, three inmates were found in a cell, all with hypodermic needles and all unconscious from drug overdoses, Mr. Horn said. They recovered, and one took another non-fatal overdose the next night.

Calling the drug trade in prison "enormously frustrating," Mr. Horn said it "gives the lie to everything we're trying to do in terms of rehabilitation."

The search had been planned since April by Mr. Horn and his staff without the knowledge of Graterford officials. In the raid, officers with drug-sniffing dogs removed inmates from their cells one at a time, searching the cells, strip-searching the inmates, and then moving to the next cell.

Officials say they might have found more drugs, but many inmates flushed them down toilets after hearing about the search.

"I suspect all of the bass and trout in the streams connected to that sewage system are jumping far out of the water," Mr. Ridge said.

Mr. Horn was realistic about the search's effect. "The minute we walk away from here, the inmates are going to start trying to figure out how to get drugs," he said.

Although few deny that Graterford has a drug problem, some prisoner advocates say the search, with all of its drama, had political motivations. The Simon case, which led to an overhaul of the state parole board, came less than a year after the release of a Pennsylvania inmate, Reginald McFadden, who went on to kill and rape on Long Island and in Rockland County, New York.

In last year's election, Mr. Ridge criticized his opponent, Lieutenant Governor Mark S. Single, for voting in favor of the McFadden parole as a member of the parole board.

Drug use at Graterford is both long-running and well-known.

"There was a period of time at Graterford that I smoked a joint when I woke up, at lunch, at dinner, and when I went to bed," said Kenneth Tervalon, 49, who was released in 1993 and says he has stopped using drugs.

Although just 10 percent of Pennsylvania's state prisoners are at Graterford, the prison accounts for 25 percent of inmate attacks on staff members and a third of inmate drug infractions, said Mr. Horn, who headed the parole system in New York State before becoming Commissioner in March.

Donald T. Vaughn, the superintendent at Graterford, said the drug problem was caused largely by its proximity to Philadelphia, which is 30 miles to the southeast. The drug market behind Graterford's 30-foot wall mirrors the city's.

Mr. Vaughn acknowledges that his staff might not have provided the "intense supervision" required for the prison. He said he had asked the corrections department for help in the past but had not yet received it.

Mr. Horn said he would leave Mr. Vaughn in charge.

With 85 percent of the inmates from Philadelphia or neighboring counties, there are frequent crowds in the visiting room, a key entry point of drugs in most prisons. Drugs packed in small balloons are passed mouth-to-mouth when inmates kiss female visitors, and inmates swallow them and pass them later. Although visitors are searched before coming in, they have been known to hide drugs in babies' diapers or in their own body cavities.

Inmates and others say Graterford has a more casual atmosphere than other prisons, which may contribute to the drug problem.

Prisoners are allowed to walk down the halls freely, not in straight lines under close supervision as is required in other prisons. And the number of volunteer workers—almost 400—gives inmates many chances to make contact with people from the outside.

"If you don't want to go to work, you just go out to the yard," said Steven Blackburn, an inmate for 12 years there until 1991. "Compared to a lot of other institutions around the state, Graterford is still considered loose."

Whatever that buys in inmate peace, it has its downside. On August 4, an inmate serving a life sentence for murder hid on a bread truck leaving the prison. He was recaptured 18 days later, but his escape was made possible because no one reported that he failed to show up for his job that day or that he was in the delivery area without authorization, Mr. Horn said.

Some inmates have been allowed to acquire enormous power. . . . A gang leader in Philadelphia has led Graterford's Muslim movement, officials said, controlling part of the prison's drug trade.

A prison guard, Lieutenant Cynthia Link, said that when the lights in the prison's mosque suddenly went out one night two years ago, the 100 inmates ignored her order to leave. Finally, one of them said, "Ms. Link, these people aren't going to move until [the gang leader] tells them to."

"I said, 'Well, go get [him], tell him I need him,'" Lieutenant Link recounted. He came, told the prisoners to leave, and they did. . . .

Editors' Note: At the time of the publication of the first edition of this book, the actual number of inmates at Graterford was over 4,000. When this article originally appeared, a portion of the prison had been shut down for repairs and emptied of inmates, considerably reducing this figure.

Appendix B

Editors' Note

Shortly after the publication of the First Edition of Life Without Parole, *Julia Cass wrote an article about Victor Hassine in* The Philadelphia Inquirer. *Cass offers salient details about the crime allegedly committed by Hassine and about his subsequent trial. She also briefly discusses how the First Edition was received by academics, Pennsylvania correctional officials, and prison inmates.*

Struggle to Survive: View From Behind Bars

Reprinted from *The Philadelphia Inquirer*, August 12, 1996
Julia Cass

BELLEFONTE, Pa.—In the 1970s, Victor Hassine toured Camp Hill state prison with classmates in a criminal justice course at Dickinson College. The sight of caged men horrified and fascinated him, but the thing he would remember for years afterward was the pool table, sitting in the center of an "honor" block for well-behaved inmates. "Jeez ... those guys must be having a blast," Hassine recalls joking to his friends. "I was incredibly naive."

Not anymore. Sixteen years into a life sentence for a 1980 Bucks County murder, Hassine is so well-acquainted with prison life—in particular, the chaotic world of Graterford—that he could write a textbook. And he has.

Published this summer and headed for college courses on penology and criminal justice, *Life Without Parole: Living in Prison Today* details Hassine's painful adjustment to incarceration. But the primary object of his lesson is that today's big prisons are "runaway trains," where both inmates and staff are struggling to survive.

Example A: Graterford.

Convicted of hiring a hit man in a drug deal gone sour, Hassine

177

spent the first five years of his sentence, from 1981 to 1986, in the state's largest maximum-security prison—the "Kingdom of Inmates," he calls it.

Going in, he had expected rigid structure. What he found, he said, was mayhem.

"Fights, stabbings and weapons were commonplace," said Hassine, 41, in an interview at Rockview state prison here, where he has been since 1989. "Prison gangs robbed with impunity. Staff smuggled in contraband. Enforcement of rules was arbitrary. It wasn't what anybody would want in a prison—or on the planet."

Hassine's book reinforces the picture that has emerged in the last year of a turbulent Graterford. In May 1995, there was the Robert "Madman" Simon scandal. Paroled from behind its walls, with the recommendation of Graterford staff, Simon then allegedly killed a New Jersey state trooper. At the legislative hearings that followed, witnesses described Graterford as violent, drug-ridden, and out of control.

Last October, state prison officials staged a massive drug and weapons raid. They transferred some staff and inmates and reduced the number of volunteers entering the prison for such programs as literacy tutoring, Bible studies and gardening.

Last spring, 10 Graterford inmates were indicted for making $2 million in illegal credit card purchases from prison telephones. So officials installed a new system restricting inmates' calls.

Hassine considers such attempts to regain control as superficial and misguided. "[Administrators have] done nothing to reduce the number of men jammed in there, and they've cut back on positive programs," he said. Instead, "what they're doing is poking a stick at the inmates."

Neither Graterford officials nor state prisons Commissioner Martin Horn had read the book and could comment, according to their representatives.

The book, however, has gotten favorable reviews in professional journals and praise from academics at schools, including the University of Scranton and Troy State University in Alabama, where it will be used.

Hassine's work is welcome because "most of the good prisoner-written books now are 20 years old, and so much has changed since then—overcrowding, budget freezes, the lean-and-mean movement, the gang bangers," said Richard A. Wright, a criminal justice professor at [Arkansas State University].

The book's harshest critics appear to be Graterford inmates. Hassine has heard they fear it will be used by state officials as reason to further tighten the reins.

"That was not my purpose," he said, "but I also think the men at Graterford should talk about what's really happening."

In Hassine's analysis, Graterford authorities began losing control in the early '80s, the beginning of a surge in the inmate population. During his confinement there, the number of men swelled from 1,900 to 2,600—750 per cell block, with a handful of guards.

The population has since grown to about 3,600.

Among the newcomers, he says, was a more aggressive and fatalistic breed of social misfit. There were the mentally ill, who commanded much of the staff's attention; the drug addicts, who would do anything to get high; and the juveniles, who became targets for rape and created havoc to attract "parental" attention.

The "older heads," Hassine says, were dismayed at the young inmates who cared more about making themselves comfortable in prison—by getting drugs and other contraband and forming gangs—than about working on their appeals and parole applications and otherwise trying to get out.

"Most of these guys have already been in and out of juvenile facilities," Hassine said, "and they've been told, 'This is your life.' "

At one point, Graterford ran out of room in the "hole"—the disciplinary unit for troublemakers and inmates who want to be protected from them. "When things got so bad that inmates couldn't even commit themselves to protective custody," Hassine said, "the population knew they had to fend for themselves."

Gangs proliferated, both for predation and protection, and guards, afraid for their own lives, usually looked the other way.

For Hassine, one of the defining moments in this inmate ascendancy came in 1983, in the "Super Bowl Sunday Chicken Riot."

First one inmate, then many more, defied the prison rules by openly bringing their chicken dinners from the C-block dining hall to their cells to eat while watching the game.

Along the way, they fought off the guards who tried to stop them. Only when the game was over, and the chicken bones were picked clean, did prison officials move to discipline some of them.

During those years, too, Graterford's underground economy grew and thrived. If he wanted his laundry done, Hassine says, he would pay an inmate laundry worker with cigarettes to have it picked up, cleaned and delivered. If he tried to send his laundry through the authorized system, he probably would not have gotten it back.

He also had at his disposal "swag men" to deliver freshly cooked food, smuggled from the kitchen, to his cell; and drugs and homemade hooch if he wanted them.

Hassine finds irony in the illegal commerce: It may have saved Graterford from becoming even more violent, for the inmates had a financial stake in some measure of peace.

An Egyptian Jew whose parents immigrated to Trenton when he was a child, Hassine took refuge in the prison's synagogue, where he helped establish halfway houses for inmates gaining release. "When you met volunteers from the outside, you were encouraged, you had a name, and whatever good values . . . you had were reinforced."

But for inmates not involved in such activities, there was a different lesson.

"Prison is a crude communism," Hassine said. "You're told, 'You're no different than anybody else.' Ambition is discouraged. They want you to do X, not less than X, but also not more than X."

Hassine's book does not detail his murder case or raise the issue of whether he deserves to be behind bars—although he has elsewhere maintained his innocence.

According to trial testimony, Hassine and his partner in a Morrisville meat market hired an acquaintance to murder a man who had gotten into a dispute with the partner over diluted drugs sold surreptitiously at the market. The hit man only wounded the intended victim but killed another man, James Puerale, who happened to be present.

The prosecutor sought the death penalty, but the jury sentenced Hassine and his partner to life in prison. In Pennsylvania, that means life without parole unless the governor commutes the sentence.

While Hassine may never escape the system, he has moved around inside it.

From Graterford, he landed in Western State Penitentiary in Pittsburgh. There, an inmate smashed his skull with a barbell, causing nerve damage that makes his left eye appear smaller than his right.

Hassine, who has a degree from New York School of Law, was a plaintiff in two lawsuits against Graterford and Western State, alleging conditions so bad they constituted cruel and unusual punishment. The inmates ultimately lost the Graterford case, although prison officials agreed to make some physical improvements. A federal judge found conditions in the Pittsburgh prison unconstitutional and ordered many changes.

Compared with Graterford and Western State, Hassine says, Rockview is calmer and more structured. He credits the preponderance of "short-timers"—inmates who are about to go home—and the warden's emphasis on education.

There, about five years ago, Hassine began writing as "a catharsis." In 1993, Thomas J. Bernard, a criminologist at nearby Pennsylvania State University, came to speak to a group of inmates, and Hassine got his card and mailed him some essays. He asked Bernard to share them with his students so they would get a more realistic view of prison life.

In Hassine's material, Bernard saw a book. "Unlike a lot of prison writing, Victor's wasn't self-serving," Bernard said. "With all the resources we are committing to prisons, I thought it would be useful to have a book that just describes what contemporary prisons are like."

Bernard showed Hassine's writings to the editor of Roxbury Publishing Co. in Los Angeles. He, too, saw a book.

Last year, Mumia Abu-Jamal, convicted of killing a Philadelphia police officer, was disciplined for writing his book, *Life From Death Row*. State prison officials said he violated the rule barring inmates from "engaging in a business or profession." A department spokesman said Hassine, unlike Abu-Jamal, isn't receiving payment. His royalties are going to the organization, Families of Murder Victims.

Hassine continues to write.

"Outsiders debate whether prisons should punish or rehabilitate," he said, "but the truth inside is: *There is no goal. . . . It's strictly survival and crisis-control.*"

From *The Philadelphia Inquirer*, August 12, 1996. Copyright © 1996 by *The Philadelphia Inquirer. The Philadelphia Inquirer* has not endorsed any point of view, any person, any enterprise, any services or products, any approach in dealing with tasks or situations, any officials or employees. Reprinted by permission.